UNDERSTANDING

HORSE
BEHAVIOR

YOUR **GUIDE** TO HORSE HEALTH
CARE AND MANAGEMENT

ISBN 1-58150-017-3

Printed in the United States of America

UNDERSTANDING

HORSE
BEHAVIOR

YOUR **GUIDE** TO HORSE HEALTH
CARE AND MANAGEMENT

By Sue McDonnell, PhD

Foreword by Dickson Varner, DVM

The Blood-Horse, Inc. Lexington, KY

Contents

FOREWORD

When we house, approach, lead, ride, drive, trailer, or breed a horse, how often do we consider the man-made transformations in that animal's inherent behavior? How do horses learn? How do horses think? Why do many horses develop behavioral problems and how can we correct these troublesome disorders? Evolution of the horse has been influenced dramatically by domestication. Yet domesticated horses and their offspring typically revert to undomesticated behavioral patterns when returned to their natural habitat.

In *Understanding Horse Behavior*, Dr. Sue McDonnell provides us with astonishing insights into horse behavior under feral conditions and translates this information into logical approaches for training/retraining horses in a domesticated setting. Indeed, Dr. McDonnell is an international authority on horse behavior. Her work in this area is widely published, and she has received numerous invitations worldwide to speak on normal and abnormal behavior of horses. Her extraordinary observation skills and perceptive reasoning have yielded a new philosophy regarding our approach to management of horses. Her research of feral horses has led to some riveting conclusions, such as the following: Stallions in bachelor bands intermingle quite well; stallions are not aggressive to foals; horses in some feral herds only drink once every one to two days; weaning is a gradual process that may not be complete until the offspring are one to three years of age; mares tend to have an 80% pregnancy rate at foal heat; mares might be bred hourly by stallions for two to three days during estrus; colts and stallions develop erections and masturbate as frequently as once every 90 minutes but rarely ejaculate; and fillies are often bred as yearlings and foal as 2-year-olds. Dr. McDonnell's work in this arena has literally revolutionized our approach to evaluation and treatment of behavioral disorders in horses.

You will be intrigued by the material presented in *Understanding Horse Behavior*. After reading and comprehending the contents, I am certain you will have a new appreciation of how we can learn from horses so that we can mold them more appropriately to meet our needs.

Dickson D. Varner, DVM, MS,
Diplomate American College of Theriogenologists
Professor and Chief of Theriogenology
Texas A&M University

INTRODUCTION

For centuries, people have been trying to understand why animals, and particularly horses, do what they do. Their behavior with one another, whether in wild populations or in domestic pastures, or even alone in a stall, intrigues most people. Do horses think? How intelligent are they? How do they survive in the wild? How do they communicate?

Similarly, one of the most beautiful inter-species relationships is that of horses and people. What do they think of us? Why do they respect us? or not? It is more often than not taken for granted that any reasonable horse or pony will abide all sorts of manipulations and engage in a variety of activities on our behalf. What we ask horses to do is often quite incompatible with the natural instincts of equids. We are surprised and frustrated when they don't. From a behaviorist's perspective, the routine work and performance feats of domestic equids are truly remarkable.

Equestrians also are usually fascinated by those people who seem to possess extraordinary ability to interact effectively with difficult horses, or to eke out the best performance in seemingly ordinary animals. Right now, interest in these specialists and in equine behavior is at an all-time high. The idea that by better understanding horse behavior we can each become more effective at training horses is everywhere in the media just now. Training workshops and clinics are almost as common as horse shows.

The goal of this book is to present current information and resources on the basics of horse behavior. Included are some examples of common behavior problems and suggested approaches to behavior modification. The topics and information are meant to be practical. A further objective is to provide some scientific perspective on horse behavior.

I am often asked, "How did you become a horse behaviorist?" Well, it wasn't because I had always wanted to, or because I just loved horses and dreamed of growing up to have a horse career. I grew up in the '50s and '60s on a dairy farm where my childhood interest in animals centered on training and fitting dairy cows for show. Although all three of us kids were involved in 4-H dairy projects, I was the family star with cattle. My brother and sister were the horse kids, for which Dad always kept a couple of horses

"Marking" jennets for field breeding studies in Brazil.

around. They were both very strong, athletic, and fearless farm kids, with a double dose of daredevil. I still have never met as smart and courageous a rider as my little red-headed sister Ruthie Ann. At no more than 10 years old, she beat me home on a pleasure ride by taking a short-cut through the apple orchards and over electric barbed wire fencing in and out of the heifer pasture. On Sunday afternoons we would set up barrels and straw bales in the dairy loafing yard for impromptu horse show/rodeo competitions. These featured neighborhood kids, horses, and dogs of all shapes and sizes in some unique events — barrel racing heats with two or three competitors on the same run, double rider, and bareback jumping classes.

It wasn't till many years after leaving the farm that I became interested in horses or their behavior. As a graduate student in psychology, I was studying learning theory — and the effects of experience on behavior. My research project was to be with rats. At the time that I was ready to begin that project, the university animal facilities were under major renovation, which meant an indefinite postponement of rat work. I casually complained about this to my next door neighbor, Linda, who had been helping me out with child care while I was going back to school. Her husband was Dr. John Hurtgen, an equine veterinarian at New Bolton Center. This is the large animal teaching and research hospital of the University of Pennsylvania School of Veterinary Medicine. John suggested that rather than studying the effects of experience on rat sexual behavior, I should consider the real world problem of sexual behavior dysfunction in horse stallions. He told me how veterinary medicine could only go so far when it came to behavior, that they really needed someone to focus on stallion behavioral problems. I assured him that it would be unlikely that I could study horses for my graduate project. After all, Dr. Ed Pollak was my major advisor. He had been trained by a student of Frank Beach, the grandfather of the formal study of sexual behavior of animals. Ed knew all about rats, and was beginning to study fish models, but knew nothing about stallions.

In the meantime, I told John that I'd love to visit New Bolton Center and see how horses breed. John invited both Ed and me out for an afternoon, and showed us a pretty important stallion with a breeding behavior problem. Good fertility when he would breed, but most of the time just not interested. How could they be sure this was just a behavioral problem, and how could they treat it? Ed said that he could help us get started, and guide us through the theoretical aspects. Within a week we were underway on adapting methods of studying sexual behavior in rats and mice to studying sexual behavior in the stallion.

Eighteen years and many mentors and students later, we are still learning more about stallion sexual behavior, as well as about horse behavior in general. Much of what we have learned has made a positive difference for the horse industry. Some of what we have done has contributed to understanding of mammals in general, including humans. People all over the world have provided opportunities to study equids, from Przewalski horses and zebras to donkeys and wild horses. And every new opportunity is fascinating. We have created a semi-feral herd of ponies here at New Bolton Center, so that we can study their behavior and physiology year round. We can follow animals from birth through maturity, study the overall social structure of the herd, and at the same time measure corresponding physiological events.

So although I didn't intend to make a career of studying horses, or follow a planned course, it has been and continues to be a very satisfying career. The best part is time spent simply watching horses.

Sue M. McDonnell
Head, Equine Behavior Program
New Bolton Center
University of Pennsylvania

CHAPTER 1

Normal Horse Behavior

BEHAVIOR OF FREE-RANGING HORSES

Most of what is known about the natural social organization and behavior of horses has come from the study of populations of feral horses throughout the world. Feral horses are those whose ancestors or who themselves were domestic stock, but have been free-running for some time. These are animals which have escaped from domestic herds or were simply turned out. Feral horse populations thrive in a number of habitats, including coastal islands of North America, the Pryor Mountains of Montana, the deserts of Western United States and Australia, and the Toi Cape of Japan. There are also a number of managed or semi-feral populations of equids throughout the world whose behavior has been studied. These are domestic or feral horses kept on relatively small preserves and whose breeding and population are relatively closely managed. A basic review of natural social organization and behavior of horses is a useful background for understanding behavior of horses in domestic conditions.

SOCIAL ORGANIZATION

Under free-running conditions, horses organize principally into breeding bands known as harems and all-male non-breeding groups known as bachelor bands. Harem bands usually include one mature breeding stallion, known as the harem stallion, and several mature mares and their immature offspring. Harems are relatively stable, long-lasting family associations. Bachelor bands vary considerably in size, from two to as many as 15 or 20 stallions which are associated most of the time. Various harem and bachelor bands of a population share home ranges and resources, but the adults do not often commingle among bands. Home ranges vary considerably in size and are logically affected by the availability of forage, shade, shelter, and water as well as population densities. A horse in an island population might have an average home range of less than one square mile, while one in a desert population might use an area as large as 10 square miles.

AT A GLANCE

- In the wild, horses organize into breeding bands known as harems and all-male groups known as bachelor bands.

- Free-ranging horses spend as much as 80% of their time foraging.

- In the wild, weaning can take up to three years.

- Harem stallions play a role in parenting.

- When turned out, domestic horses organize and interact like their free-ranging counterparts.

MAINTENANCE BEHAVIOR AND TIME BUDGETS

Maintenance behavior includes feeding, drinking, elimination, grooming, and rest necessary for ongoing survival of the individual. Free-ranging horses spend most of their time — an estimated 50% to 80% — foraging. Season, weather conditions, and vegetation density appear to affect the variation. For example, most herds stop grazing and seek shelter during a heavy driving rainstorm. Extremes in seasonal temperatures also can interrupt grazing.

Loafing or standing rest and recumbent rest together comprise the next greatest amount of the time budget of free-ranging horses. Loafing and rest usually account for about 20% to 30% of the time budget. Standing horses can go into a heavily drowsy state or even light sleep. This is possible because of a unique leg joint and muscle configuration called a *stay apparatus*, that enables the horse to lock the joints into a weight-bearing position with little effort. This is a particularly adaptive ability that allows for quick flight from danger. Deep sleep occurs only during recumbency, usually full lateral recumbency.

In most natural habitats water is not readily available throughout the grazing area, and might be a limited resource shared by many bands within a home range. Trekking to a water site and drinking is almost always done as a herd, and often at a particular time of day. Horses generally go to water once a day or once every two days, although longer intervals have been observed. Where water is readily available in their grazing areas, horses may drink small amounts more frequently. They drink from streams, lakes, water holes, or puddles.

Mutual grooming between bachelor stallions.

In natural environments horses tend to seek natural shelters and in some instances seem to create shelter by hollowing out natural vegetation. The preferred shelter is often on a ridge with good visibility and quick escape possibilities, and with protection from prevailing wind. To escape heat and insects, horses have been observed to forage out breezy sheds in thickets.

Self-grooming is an ongoing activity which varies with season and weather. During springtime shedding and biting insect conditions, self-grooming is interspersed with grazing and loafing. Specific grooming behaviors include scratching and rubbing against objects, scratching various areas of the head and fore body with a hind leg, as well as nipping at limbs and accessible body parts. Rolling on the ground also appears to serve a grooming function. It is usually done at the end of each recumbent rest. Stallions also roll as an apparent inter-male ritual. This is often done at specific rolling sites that become "dust bowls" after repeated use.

Within a band of horses, all of the adults tend to engage in particular maintenance activities simultaneously — so they graze at the same time, rest together as a group, trek to water together, and so on. This is true for both harem and bachelor bands. It often seems that a dominant mare within a harem band or a dominant bachelor within a bachelor band takes the lead on changing activities. When a

A harem stallion enjoying a roll in the water hole.

group of horses is resting together, it is typical for one or two in the group to remain standing in a higher level of alertness, as if serving as sentinels.

Horses show no particular pattern of maintenance behaviors throughout the day and night — they graze around the clock and rest at various times throughout the day and night. There might be periods of the day during which some activities increase in apparent logical association with weather conditions. For example, during hot summer afternoons herds might spend a greater percentage of time loafing in the shade and become more active in the cool evenings or in the early mornings. Play fighting behavior in bachelor bands and for play among juveniles often occurs at the same time as sudden changes in weather, either from hot to cool in the summer or from very cold to warm in the winter.

Recumbent rest occurs at all times throughout the day and night, but the longest periods of recumbent rest are usually during the early morning hours before dawn.

COMMUNICATION

It is evident from the stability and coordinated activities of bands and herds of horses that quite elaborate communication is ongoing among individuals and groups. All senses seem to be involved in communication among individuals. Certainly very subtle visual cues from body, head, and ear positions as well as facial expressions are important aspects of communication among individuals. Humans probably have a very minimal appreciation of the ongoing visual communication among horses.

Auditory communication among horses includes a variety of specific vocalizations, grunts, and other sounds produced by the animal including hoof sounds. During inter-male posturing episodes and aggressive interactions, the sound produced by stomping seems to be an element of the communication among the participants.

The behavior of equids also suggests considerable olfactory (smell) communication concerning the identity and rank of individuals. Breath odor, urine, feces, and other body odors all seem to receive considerable attention, both by sniffing behavior, and in certain circumstances by a subsequent flehmen (lip curling) response. The horse has a relatively well-developed accessory olfactory system which includes a second sensory organ of smell known as the vomeronasal organ. Small ducts in the nose lead to this organ which is thought to be able to detect social odors known as pheromones. The flehmen response is thought to draw fluids into the vomeronasal organ.

Tactile communication is also evident. As animals meet or pass, they often reach out with the head to touch. Tactile cues are also an obvious part of communication between mares and their foals, among stallions and mares during courtship and mating, and in initiation of play among foals. Juveniles touch one another and touch adults at a much higher rate than do adults.

DEVELOPMENT

Foals are precocious young. That means that they are well developed behaviorally very soon after birth. Foals stand and nurse within the first hour of life. Within the first day they run, play, explore, groom, and keep up with the herd. Their behavioral repertoire is nearly as complete as that of a yearling. The percentage of time spent resting and nursing is greatest in the neonate and gradually declines with age. Play is initially solitary. Almost all foals play in a characteristic fashion of running circles around their dam, often first in one

direction and then reversing for several circles in the opposite direction. The diameter of the circles usually grows daily through about two weeks of age. At about two weeks of age foals then typically run off in one

Young foals appear to enjoy each other's company.

direction or another, often seeming to test the amount of distance their dam or harem stallion will tolerate before threatening or retrieving them. Youngsters within a harem seem especially interested in each other and from a few days of age associate with other foals and yearlings within the group. They can engage in running play from a few days of age. The young of different harems also might seem drawn to each other and commingle between their harems whenever the opportunities arise.

Among horses living in the wild, weaning is a prolonged and gradual process that typically begins sometime between six to 12 months of age and might not be complete for two or three years. In most instances, there seems to be reduced nursing when a subsequent sibling arrives. For the rare mares that do not conceive for a season, their foal typically is not weaned until much later. But yearling, 2-year-old, and even older offspring have been observed to nurse their dam occasionally, even after a subsequent foal arrives. The nursing by older offspring seems acceptable to the dam.

LEAVING THE NATAL BAND

As female offspring mature, they leave their natal band to join existing harem bands or to form a new harem with a bachelor. During the transition from the natal band to a harem, a young filly temporarily might attach to a bachelor band or travel with a band of juveniles in transition. As male offspring mature, they leave their natal bands to join existing bachelor bands or form new bachelor bands. Young males in transition may travel alone or with a band of juveniles in transition. Both fillies and colts may come and go from the natal band, staying days to weeks with and away from the natal band before finally leaving.

DOMINANCE AND LEADERSHIP

Dominance hierarchies in terms of access to resources are evident both among individuals within a band and among various bands. This is most obvious at limited resource sites, for example at watering holes, insect-refuge sites, and shady resting areas. Bands will drink in a strict order and individuals within a band typically will drink in an established order. Older animals generally dominate younger animals. Leadership of a harem band is shared between the harem stallion and usually an older, dominant mare. The harem stallion usually directs the movement and protection of the band when threatened by a neighboring band. A dominant mare tends to lead the movement and routine activity changes of the band during times of quiet maintenance. The dominant mare tends to lead at the head of a line of band members. When the stallion is directing movement he is typically at the rear of the band.

Foals and juveniles are generally submissive to adults. A characteristic posture of submission includes mouth movements known as champing or snapping. Many people who see this behavior interpret it as exaggerated sucking movements to convey a message to the adult that, "I'm just a baby, don't hurt me."

AGGRESSIVE BEHAVIOR

Horses at liberty spend very little time in frank aggressive encounters. Most limited resources such as water holes, shade, shelter, or dust bathing sites are controlled by already established dominance orders or by relatively subtle threats rather

Aggressive behavior of harem stallions.

than overt aggression. Stallions appear aggressively threatening when herding their harem or retrieving a stray mare or juvenile, but this also takes the form of a threatening posture and driving behavior that typically involves little direct contact. Harem stallions which encounter one another engage in ritualized posturing and fighting that involves charging, rearing, boxing, kicking, and biting usually at the flanks, neck, shoulder, crest, and legs. Bachelor stallions engage in intermittent, sparring aggres-

Bachelor stallions wrestling.

sion that rarely accelerates into frank aggression.

BONDS AND AFFILIATIONS

Within harem bands, the strongest bonds appear to be those of mares with their foals, the stallion with each mare, the stallion with foals, some individual pairs of mares, and the older

Bachelor stallions form strong alliances.

juveniles with each other. Evidence of bonds among individuals includes protectiveness in the case of dams with their foals and of stallions with their mares and foals, spatial association, and mutual grooming. When the herd is loafing on hot summer afternoons, closely bonded pairs often stand head to tail alongside one another so that their swishing tails effectively move air and keep flies from each other's head. In terms of reaction to separation, the strongest bonds seem to be those of harem stallions with individual mares, and those of foals and their dams.

The behavior of stallions within bachelor bands also suggests strong affiliations and alliances. Preferred associations of two or three stallions are common within bachelor bands. Much of their behavior, for example, play fighting, mutual grooming, and inter-male sexual behavior, suggests strong trust among individuals. Bachelors can form alliances to steal a mare or to displace a harem stallion. Typically one of the team which stole a mare or a harem of mares then turns on his partner or partners and keeps the mares for himself.

As with any non-human species, it is difficult to access the extent to which animals experience emotions that humans associate with family bonds. It is easy to anthropomorphise when we see a mare lingering near a dead foal, or a closely bonded bachelor pair. But at present we really don't know the extent to which animals feel grief or love or camaraderie as understood by humans.

REPRODUCTIVE BEHAVIOR

In feral herds, the majority of foaling and breeding is in spring and summer, although births have been observed year round. Most mares have a foaling interval of approximately one year. Estimates are that more than 80% become pregnant on the postpartum estrus within two weeks after foaling. Nearly all of the remaining 20% become pregnant on the second estrus after foaling, by six weeks after foaling. For most mares which have a foal every year, then, the normal state throughout her life is pregnancy, with only about two to five weeks per year non-pregnant.

The estrus period itself lasts about three to five days. When a mare is in estrus the stallion becomes particularly vigilant and protective of his harem, lingering nearby the estrous mare. Most mares go through a stage of ambivalence, in which they appear attractive to the stallion, but they are not yet willing to stand for breeding. Once the mare starts standing for breeding, it is usually quite frequent, as often as once per hour or more for two or three consecutive days.

Mares and stallions normally continue to be reproductively active and fertile throughout life. Harem stallions can hold their harem for many years, so are active reproductively and fertile in the wild as late as into their 20s.

If nutrition is good, fillies mature and start breeding by about one year of age, foaling then at about two. If nutrition is poor, they might not become pregnant until the following spring. Young fillies might breed while still in their natal band, but usually not with the harem stallion. It is often reported that young colts or bachelor band stallions may be tolerated to breed these young fillies. The fillies also may leave their natal band for short periods when in estrus and return to the natal band. This is likely a natural incest avoidance mechanism.

PARENTAL-FOAL BEHAVIOR

Within the last few hours before parturition the mare seems to try to stay off in a quiet area away from other harems, and could begin to repel any herd mates that approach. The stallion also often appears to play a role in keeping extra distance between the harem and other horses. The early, immediate care of the foal is done by the dam. Mares display maternal behavior toward the foal within seconds after delivery, including nuzzling, licking, avoiding walking or lying on the neonate, allowing and facilitating nursing, and protecting the foal by positioning herself between the newborn and intruders, and even attacking or driving away intruders.

Interactive bonding behavior occurs between neonate and dam beginning at parturition and continuing for the first day or two until the secure bond is established. The foal plays an active role in eliciting maternal behavior and bonding. Even

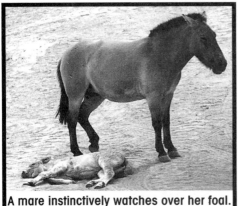

before standing, the foal will reach out with the head and neck to nudge and nose the dam. The foal will vocalize and respond to the vocalizations of the dam, even before standing. After standing the foal will seek the udder. Once on its feet and nursing the foal will actively linger near and return to the mare if separated. The foal also

A mare instinctively watches over her foal.

seems instinctively to stay on the far side of the dam, away from a potential threat. This natural tendency makes it frustrating to get a quick photo of a neonatal foal on the near side.

The birth and the neonatal foal seem to be a curiosity to the herd. Siblings, other foals and yearlings, other mares in the harem, and the stallion all appear drawn to the birthing and to the neonate. For the first one to three days, the dam typically threatens others away from the foal. For the first two or three weeks, the dam is usually the most frequent nearest neighbor. Normally, both the mare and the foal work at maintaining proximity, but pairs vary considerably in whether it is the dam or the foal which "worries" most about separation or works hardest to maintain proximity. Young, primiparous mares sometimes seem lax in their maternal duties, in which case the foal can seem especially watchful and careful to stay with the dam.

Through the first month of age the foal begins to lengthen its range from the dam, who seems to relax her vigilance. At the same time, it seems to be the harem stallion that, in fact, takes on a good portion of the "parenting" behavior. This includes playing with the foals and yearlings, staying with the young play groups when they wander or play short distances from the mares, and retrieving them from straying off too far from the herd.

BEHAVIOR OF DOMESTIC HORSES

The behavior of domestic horses varies considerably with the various housing and management practices. On one extreme, some horses are kept in virtual isolation in darkened and/or climate-controlled cage-like stalls bedded with shavings and fed diets of mostly grain and little roughage. Their behavior is logically limited by physical constraints and social isolation. On the other extreme, many domestic horses are outside all or most of the time with other horses, and their daily time budgets and range of behaviors can be quite similar to that of a wild equid.

The maintenance behavior of horses kept at pasture is often quite similar to that of free-running horses. Horses usually are not kept in breeding groups that can organize into tightly grouped harem or bachelor bands. Nonetheless assemblages of mares tend to behave as a unit as would mares in a harem. Sometimes a gelding more or less performs the role of a harem stallion in keeping the mares together in a tight band. No matter what the grouping it is typical for all of the horses within an enclosure to interact as a herd. They are usually performing the same maintenance activities as a group, and maintaining proximity within the enclosure.

For horses stabled all or most of the time, their behavioral time budgets logically reflect their diet. When hay is not continuously available and when grain is fed, the time budget typically shifts in the direction of a greater proportion of time spent standing at rest and less time eating. Drinking in stabled horses is usually associated with eating hay. So if a horse is given hay twice daily, most if not all drinks will be taken during or soon after hay is consumed.

Continuously stabled horses typically have little or no direct social interaction with other horses, so have an obvious void in social behavior in their time budgets. Stallions are almost always kept from having any direct contact with other horses. Horses which are stabled, but have several hours of daily turn-out with other horses often spend as much or more time interacting with other horses than horses kept continually at pasture. This is likely due to the fact that each time they are turned out, the entire group or certain individuals seem to have to re-sort or re-confirm the order within the group, particularly if the turn-out groups vary from day to day.

The reproductive behavior of domestic horses also varies with management, but the following key differences are typical:

• breeding of most domestic horses is highly controlled

• mate selection and the time of breeding are tightly managed

• contact of the male and female is for copulation only or not at all for artificial insemination

Developmental behavior differs for domestic foals, depending again on management practices. Almost never are sires of foals included in their social group, so parenting behavior is all maternal. Where groups of mares and foals are pastured together, social play and other early developmental behavior are likely quite similar to that of horses under free-running conditions. Almost all domestic foals are weaned and separated from the dam earlier and more abruptly than would be the case under natural conditions. However, the usual domestic weaning age of three to six months corresponds with the time that most foals are naturally spending relatively little time nursing and spending most of their time socializing with other foals.

HAVE DOMESTIC HORSES LOST THEIR INSTINCTIVE BEHAVIOR?

Despite generations of selection and managed breeding, a fascinating feature of domestic horse behavior is that most when turned out immediately revert to social organization and behavior very similar to that of long-term feral horses. So, for example, a stallion from a long line of race or show stallions which has never been turned out to breed with mares will, when turned out with a group of mares, likely immediately perform normal harem formation and mainte-

nance behaviors similar to those of semi-feral stallions. If multiple stallions are turned out, one will win the position of harem stallion and the remainder will form a bachelor group. This is true even

A domestic stallion turned out with mares quickly assumes the role of the harem stallion.

for most stallions which have been kept isolated from other horses since they were yearlings and have had impoverished social developmental opportunities. This is evidence that with genetic selection for domestically desirable traits, horses have not lost important instinctive behaviors. It is also evidence that most of these behaviors do not depend significantly on developmental experience.

CHAPTER 2

Basic Temperament and Behavior

Anyone who knows a number of horses recognizes that while horses have many common characteristics, each one has unique behavior patterns and a general disposition that distinguishes it from other horses. In every culture and region of the world as well as every equine discipline and industry, there is a specific vocabulary for describing individual character or personality of horses. In English, we use terms such as bargey, bold, cautious, competitive, cooperative, forgiving, generous, honest, hot, intelligent, kind, lazy, nervous Nellies, nosy, obedient, proud, quiet, sensitive, shy, smart, steady, sour, stoic, stubborn, stupid, sweet, timid, or wise, just to name a few. It usually takes a few descriptors to sum up any one horse. We also recognize that when horses are turned out with other horses, they have distinct personalities. For example, they might be social, bossy, curious, aggressive, leaders, followers, or loners. It is not uncommon for a horse's personality to change with changes in herd composition. And owners often point out that an individual horse might have a different personality with people than it does with horses.

While personality and its development in horses has not been widely studied, it is safe to say that there are many factors that contribute. Discussion of what makes a particular personality almost always boils down to the old questions of nature, nurture, and the interactions.

BREED AND GENETICS

Those who have worked with different breeds of horses almost always have their opinion as to basic temperament and behavioral characteristics of certain breeds. Few would not agree that in general the warmblooded breeds, such as Thoroughbreds and Arabians, are generally more reactive than the more stoic, cold-blooded (draft) or pony

AT A GLANCE

• Every horse has unique behavior patterns and disposition.

• Genetics plays an important role in basic temperament and behavior.

• Studies indicate that younger horses learn more readily than older ones.

• A horse's personality remains malleable throughout life and is influenced by the people and animals around it.

breeds. Also, horse breeders have long recognized the heritability of certain basic temperaments in lines of horses and select for those characteristics when breeding. So there is no doubt that genetics plays a big role in basic temperament and behavioral characteristics of horses. While many good behavioral characteristics and problem behavioral character-

istics are heritable, they are probably not highly heritable. For example, a stallion with a tendency to savage people is probably more likely to have some male offspring born with that tendency than a stallion which does not savage people. But the

The "warmblood" breeds like Thoroughbreds are generally more reactive.

Draft breeds usually have quiet temperaments.

savage stallion is also likely to have many male offspring which do not have the tendency. The same is true of the tendency for positive traits; there are no guarantees.

GENDER

Probably the broadest generalizations concerning basic equine temperament and behavior involve comparisons of mares, stallions, and geldings. Stallions, of course, are intact males. The majority of equestrians would not consider keeping or using a stallion for other than breeding. A stallion is typically very strong physically, and strong willed. If not trained when and where to breed, a stallion will instinctively respond sexually whenever the occasion arises. In most equine athletic disciplines, those who prefer to work with stallions usually appreciate the strength and competitive drive of an intact male horse. For such experienced handlers or trainers, the

Stallions are typically strong and strong-willed.

sexual and aggressive behavior of a stallion is remarkably well controlled with simple behavior modification. The key to success with stallions appears to be firm, consistent, judicious, and skillful training. While physical size and strength can help, it is certainly not necessary for handling and training stallions. In fact, trying to control a stallion with brute strength alone is usually futile.

A rowdy performing stallion actually might benefit from the opportunity to breed. Providing clear signals that distinguish breeding time and performing time can help most stallions learn and abide by the difference. In other words, for some stallions, it appears easier for them to suppress their sexual behavior if they actually have a time and place where it is allowed and encouraged.

Normal stallion behavior also poses housing and general management challenges. Stallions are usually pastured, housed, and transported separately from other horses. Beyond the obvious reasons of preventing sexual interaction and breeding, this is done to avoid wear and tear on the stallion as he will try to whatever extent possible to perform normal harem stallion behavior. This includes pacing fence lines and stalls, and trying to fight off other males.

Mares and geldings are more popular choices for performance horses in general than stallions. Geldings tend to be less aggressive, perhaps less distracted by other horses, and easier to house and transport than stallions. However, castration, regardless of the age or previous sexual experience, does not always eliminate all stallion-like behavior. If given the opportunity, as many as half of geldings will show stallion-like behavior to mares, many will herd mares, and even mount and appear to breed. Similarly, while castration does tend to "mellow" most

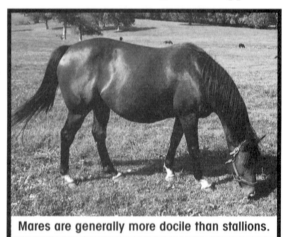

Mares are generally more docile than stallions.

horses, it does not eliminate general misbehavior. Traditional behavior modification is usually much more effective in controlling sexual and aggressive behavior in a gelding under saddle or in-hand than it is with an intact stallion. For example, in most cases it is easier to eliminate biting behavior in a gelding than in an intact stallion. Also, treatment aimed at quieting sexual and aggressive behavior, such as progesterone, is typically more effective in geldings than in intact stallions. This stands to reason, because the actual male hormones from the testicle that increase the sexual and aggressive motivation in a stallion are not present in the gelding.

Mares, like geldings, are generally more docile than stallions. The one common complaint about mare temperament and behavior is specific problems and inconsistencies in performance related to their estrus cycle. These are described in detail in Chapter 7.

With gender, like many factors that seem to affect equine temperament and behavior, there certainly is an interactive effect of people. People who like and appreciate stallions, for example, seem to really bring out the best in a stallion. They seem to develop a mutual respect. The same is true for those who like to work with mares. There are some people who always ride mares and never seem to complain of estrus cycle-related performance problems.

AGE

Age of a horse is almost always confounded with experience and training, so it is difficult to evaluate effects of age on basic temperament. However, there are some generalizations that can be made. Most young horses are more curious, playful, and reactive than mature horses. Scientific studies indicate that younger horses learn more readily than mature horses. They likely adapt more readily to changes in physical and social environment as well. Most very old horses are more "sensible," quiet, and even more docile than young or middle-aged horses. Of course, this impression might simply be the result that only nice horses are kept into old age.

HANDLING AND ENVIRONMENT

In the whole scheme of things, the critical factors in most aspects of domestic horse temperament and behavior are their management, environment, and particularly their interaction with people. People with lots of horse behavior problems don't like to hear this, and most people with lots of behavior-problem-free horses know this very well. The personality of most horses remains somewhat plastic throughout life, and it is greatly affected by the animals and people around it. Probably horses are most affected by their first han-

Initial handling can make an impression.

dling experiences when young, but even aged horses can be affected by how they are handled. It is not at all uncommon for sequential owners or trainers of a particular horse to describe it quite differently. Even within the same time period, a horse can show very different attributes depending on the people or environment around it. Honest trainers often admit personality or environmental conflicts, and recognize that a particular horse might do better with another trainer or in a more quiet or more active stable.

CHAPTER 3

Horse "Intelligence" and Thinking

HOW INTELLIGENT ARE HORSES?

Behavioral scientists usually address questions of animal intelligence by evaluating and comparing the learning ability of various species. Specific types of learning have been defined objectively, and individual or species abilities in each type of learning can be estimated in experiments cleverly customized for every type of organism, from very simple single-cell organisms to complex mammals.

HABITUATION AND SENSITIZATION

Habituation can get a horse used to a stimulus.

Habituation is the process of gradually reducing an instinctive reaction to a repeated stimulus that has no particular consequence. In other words, getting used to a stimulus. A new insect zapper goes off and the horses in nearby stalls are startled and retreat to the back of their stalls. Within two days, they hardly flinch when it goes off. This is probably the most common type of learning in a young foal, and it continues through life. Initially, a young foal or a mature horse in a new environment reacts to almost all stimuli. So simple sounds, movements, touch, or strange objects elicit a startle or escape reaction, or at least a cautious investigation. An important part of life is to sort out the meaningful from the non-meaningful, particularly the harmful from the non-harmful aspects of the environment and to investigate or react only when necessary.

Sensitization is almost the opposite of habituation in that it involves becoming more reactive or responsive to a stimulus as a result of experience. A common example of sensitization is the once curious and compliant horse becomes fearful and seemingly hyperreactive to a particular person who has caused it pain.

AT A GLANCE

- Horses learn by association and reinforcement, both positive and negative.

- Observation does not help a horse to learn a particular task.

- Horses can "learn to learn."

- Horses can remember what they learned even if years have elapsed since they performed a particular task.

- There is little evidence to suggest that horses are capable of higher mental processes.

ASSOCIATIVE LEARNING

Horses are excellent learners of associations between events and contingencies, both positive and negative. This is the basis of most of their learning about their environment and then their training for work. A day-old foal which is bottle fed quickly learns stimuli associated with feeding. It will initiate sucking movement at the sight of the bottle, then at the sight of the person holding the bottle, and maybe at words spoken to the foal while the feeding is being prepared. This type of learning is known as classical conditioning. Learned or conditioned stimuli (sight of a bottle) become able to elicit unlearned or natural responses (sucking movements).

Operant conditioning is a second main type of associative learning. This involves learning the relationship between some action and its consequences, and altering the likelihood or strength of the action accordingly. The foal nips his mom while nursing, then mom kicks or nips the foal on the butt. The foal usually stops nipping, showing evidence that he has learned the negative consequence of his nipping and has modified his behavior accordingly. A negative consequence of an action is called a punishment; it reduces the likelihood of the recurrence of the action. A positive consequence is called reinforcement; it increases the likelihood of the action. If instead of kicking the foal the dam nuzzled the foal each time it nipped her, the nipping would likely increase in frequency or strength.

A positive outcome or reinforcement can take two forms. It can be application of a positive event or stimulus (nuzzling) or it can be the termination of a negative stimulus. For

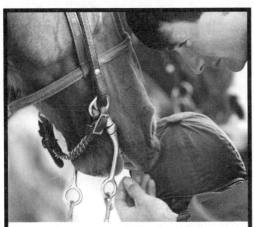

Horses learn more efficiently with positive reinforcement.

example, the dam lifts a hind leg in a threat to kick the foal each time it approaches, and only relaxes her leg when the foal nurses gently and doesn't nip. The cessation of the threat to kick would be a negative reinforcement for gentle, non-nipping nursing behavior by the foal. The term aversive conditioning refers to use of negative stimuli, that is, negative reinforcement or punishment. Positive reinforcement-based training refers to using principally positive reinforcement and no aversive stimuli to shape behavior. For most complex tasks, animals learn more efficiently with positive reinforcement as opposed to aversive conditioning.

For animals to learn operant associations the consequences must be very closely linked in time to the action. Both rewards and punishments must be immediate in order for the horse to understand the connection. In the case of punishment of an undesirable behavior, it is best if the behavior itself is interrupted by the negative consequence. This is one area where often well-meaning trainers make costly mistakes. My favorite example is the halter horse trainer who after an unsuccessful class takes his horse out back and "gets into him." That horse will have no idea that the punishment had anything to do with the class. More likely, the association made with the negative consequence will be with walking behind arenas, or following obediently behind this person, with the person himself, or something else more closely associated in time with the negative experience. Because of such timing difficulties, punishment is often ineffective, and even counterproductive. In fact, there are very few tasks that performance horses need to learn for which punishment is more effective than positive reinforcement. The principle that reinforcement-based learning is much more efficient than punishment-based learning is just now being widely appreciated by the general public involved in animal training.

Two relatively complex associative learning abilities that have been demonstrated in horses are temporal and spatial reversals. The test of such ability is usually done with feed bins. The task is to learn to make the correct choice (the bin with the feed) on the first try. Horses can learn that the correct choice simply alternates from one bin to the other each time, say black bin-white bin-black bin-white bin. They also can learn that the correct choice alternates by spatial position, say left position-right position. They can learn to disregard the color and pay attention to the position. Actually, horses seem particularly clever at learning and remembering spatial positions.

Horses can learn what are called schedules of reinforcement. For example, horses quite readily learn to press a lever so many times (fixed ratio) or at certain time intervals (fixed interval) to get a treat. Horses also are extremely good at distinguishing very subtle stimuli or cues. This includes subtle differences in shapes, patterns, sizes, etc. This is why we sometimes accuse a horse of reading our mind. "He knows I am going to give him a shot!" Horses actually can detect our anticipatory changes in body posture or expression that we might not even perceive ourselves. This allows a horse to respond accordingly even before we perceive that we have made an overt signal.

Horses also are very good at learning secondary reinforcement or punishment. Treats or painful physical punishment are primary reinforcements, that is they naturally have positive or negative value to the horse. Other stimuli repeatedly paired with primary reinforcement take on the quality of the stimuli with which they are paired. So specific words or voice tone paired with treats or with physical discipline quickly become meaningful secondary reinforcement or punishment.

Counter-conditioning is a term for a method to eliminate an undesirable behavior by teaching a substitute behavior that precludes the undesirable behavior. It works very well in training horses. Say a horse on a lead has a tendency to rush ahead of the handler or to circle around the handler. One way to stop the rushing and circling is to train the horse in a separate lesson to back up to a verbal or visual command. Then each time the horse rushes forward as it is being led, the "back" command can be given. The horse cannot simultaneously go forward and go back, hence the term counter-conditioning. After a few times, the horse appears to learn that rushing past the handler results in having to back up a bit. The net result is that the horse will begin walking along at a desirable pace. Counter-conditioning can be a very peaceful substitute for punishment, which with some horses, provokes playful battle that gets you nowhere.

SOCIAL LEARNING

Social learning or imitation involves the acquisition of behavior simply by observing that behavior in another. Studies have been conducted in which horses have been allowed first to observe other horses learning a task and then were taught the task. Those allowed to observe others first were no better at learning the task than those that were not given the opportunity to observe. In watching young foals at pasture, I have observed instances of foals in play with objects in which it seemed that foals "copied" actions of other foals after observation.

LATENT LEARNING

The term latent learning comes from studies in which a recently fed rat was allowed to explore a maze containing a food reward. So the rat would find the food, but not consume the reward, nor change its behavior in the maze at that time. Then on a later occasion when the rat was hungry, it would be returned to the maze to measure whether it would appear to remember where the food was and hurry to find it. There is no evidence that horses learn in this fashion.

INSIGHT LEARNING

Insight learning is the term used to describe the "aha" or "light bulb going off" experience, or the learning that involves thinking through a problem and solving it without any actual physical trial-and-error experience. As with any animal, we can really only guess as to the complexity of horses' cognitive abilities. Currently we don't have proof one way or the other with horses, but it is unlikely that they are capable of insight learning.

LEARNING TO LEARN

A fascinating feature of animal and human learning is the phenomenon of "learning to learn." That is, once we have been presented with learning tasks, learning efficiency on subsequent new tasks is improved. It's as if we learn that the rules or even the game changes, and so we become better at expecting, detecting, and learning those changes. Horses do clearly learn to learn. We see this phenomenon over and over again with horses and ponies that are a part of our university research herd. For example, a pony stallion is selected for his first experiment in which he has to do a certain set of tasks before getting the opportunity to breed a mare. In this first experiment we are always impressed with the steep learning curve. By day three or four, most pony stallions have learned and willingly comply with the various procedures.

When an experiment ends, there is often a month or more before the pony may be assigned to a new experiment. First, it is always fascinating how many conditioned stimuli and procedures from the first experiment are retained. But it is usually the case that the procedures for the new experiment are different from the first experiment, and the stallion has to learn the new procedures. With each successive experiment, it is obvious that the pony is quicker to give up his learned procedures from previous experiments and also quicker to take on new learned behaviors. It also is clear that he expects to have to do something before he is allowed to breed, and he just waits for our direction so that he can comply and get on to his reward. These "old pros" often learn the experimental protocol on the first day. So on the second day they lead the experimenter from station to station in the correct order for pre-breeding measures or procedures. This all means then that horses can learn a concept.

Before getting carried away with horses learning concepts, though, I need to share the story of one of my favorite horse learning studies. It was reported in 1911 by G. V. Hamilton, who was comparing animal species on what was called trial-and-error learning, or exploring alternative solutions. It concerned the concept of exploring alternate exits from an enclosure. A horse was familiarized with an area and each of four similar exit doors. The horse then was given a series of trials in which two of the doors were locked and two would open if pushed. The horse focused most of its effort at just one particular location, as if failing to learn the concept of "exit door," or trying alternative options. For those who have had the opportunity to work with other farm species as well as with horses, it is no surprise that horses do so poorly on these trial-and-error tests. A related concept which horses are slow to learn is that of the "detour." A gate along a fence line can be wide open, and quite familiar to a horse. But if the rest of the herd is on the opposite side of the fence and has moved up the fence away from the gate, the separated horse seems unable to find the gate. It will often frantically run or even jump the fence nearest the rest of the herd before moving along the fence line to remember or find the open gate. Those who have walked mares with foals trailing behind know this problem very well.

HORSE MEMORY

Another measure of intelligence is the ability to retain what is learned. Horses do very well at remembering specific tasks, associations, discriminations, or reversals that they have learned. So for example, a trained driving horse that has been turned out to pasture for months or years without being driven, or that has been used as a riding horse and not driven for long periods, is likely to perform reasonably well when initially returned to harness.

Horses remember what they learn.

Horses often even retain response to specific voice commands and subtle physical cues for years.

INTELLIGENCE TESTS

I don't know of any formal testing of horse intelligence. However, it is easy to rank horses on the outcome of any of these learning and memory tasks as a basis of selection for a particular work or performance career. The closest to formal application of testing of equine learning ability are certain aspects of the 100-day performance tests of various breeds of warmbloods in which horses are schooled and tested under relatively controlled conditions. While many other aspects of temperament, conformation, and athletic ability are considered in these tests, they do likely test the relative ability of horses to learn specific tasks.

HOW DO HORSES THINK?

It is only within the last decade or so that behavioral scientists have seriously accepted and explored the possibility of higher mental processes in animals. Cognition, or the capacity for mental processing, problem solving, mental modeling, and abstract thinking is much more difficult to measure and compare among species. Most of the work has focused on primates, so very little can be said about cognitive abilities of farm animals. The little evidence available in horses suggests that their capacity for higher mental processes is very limited, and that most of their behavior can be accounted for with instinctual stimulus response patterns and modifications resulting from simple learning processes.

In the practice of working with horses and other pets, it seems that the trend is to attribute a more and more complex cognitive ability to animals, with little or no scientific evidence. For example, it is no longer the extreme exception among experienced and reasonable horse owners to believe that their horse can entertain abstract thought, think in language, or be manipulative, sneaky, or insightful. "They're taking me to a horse show tomorrow, and I don't like going to shows without my old pal Star, so I think I'll colic so I can stay home." Many people today are actually paying animal psychics to read a horse's mind and thoughts by long-distance mental telepathy, and seem to believe the elaborate explanations of horse's inner thoughts. Some animal communicators even offer to send an owner's messages to their horse by mental telepathy. Every serious horse behaviorist I know who understands the mechanisms of learning and cognition will say they really have no evidence that horses have much cognitive ability.

There is no evidence that horses understand time, in the sense of past, present, and future. There is no evidence that horses are aware of their existence, have a mental concept of life or death, have a mental concept of family or relatedness. Horses might understand a few simple words spoken in consistent tones, as conditioned stimuli, but

Horses probably have a limited capacity for higher mental processes.

likely understand nothing of the meaning of what people say. What this means is that all equine behavior can be explained in terms of innate behavior and simple types of learning without advanced cognitive representation of the world.

These comments may seem highly philosophical, and a bit out of order in light of so little scientific evidence in the horse. But from a practical viewpoint, it seems that many more mistakes in interacting with and managing the behavior of animals are made by over-estimating rather than by under-estimating their intelligence. I find that often the happiest and most productive animal-human relationships are the result of a realistic understanding of the basic behavior of the animal, a clear grasp of how that animal can and cannot learn, and consistent training and interaction according to the simplest learning principles. This approach puts most of the responsibility on the people interacting with the animal rather than on the animal. Asking, "What am I doing to cause this behavior?" or "What can I do to change this behavior?" is almost always more productive than proclaiming "Stupid animal!"

CHAPTER 4

Special Training and Handling Methods

Most people working with horses develop systematic methods for routine handling and training, correcting problem behaviors, and teaching others how to handle horses. A number of these methods for handling or training horses have been organized and promoted nationally and internationally in videos, books, and road clinics. When reduced to the basics, the various methods turn out to be very similar. The relative effectiveness and popularity of any of these techniques lies more in the simplicity and clarity of communication of the technique rather than in the specific technique itself. The most popular horse handling and training techniques of recent years have the following principles in common:

• gentle handling, as opposed to a rough and rowdy approach

• systematic desensitization

• primarily positive and negative reinforcement to shape behavior

• recognition and incorporation of the equine's natural behavioral tendencies

• submission response-based progression of training

• positive interaction such as grooming or massage, independent of training goals

• untested claims of particular effectiveness of certain training aids, specific actions, or sequences.

EARLY INTENSIVE HANDLING OF FOALS

A particularly interesting technique that has been promoted over the last decade is intensive early handling of foals. The most widely promoted method of intense early handling of foals is known as *imprint training*, developed by a California veterinarian, Dr. Robert Miller. The technique involves handling and thorough systematic desensitization done as early as possible on the day of birth. Systematic desensitization is the repeated presentation of initially mildly aversive stimuli until the stimuli are tolerated. The massage technique used with foals involves repeating sets of a fixed number of rhythmic, gentle squeezings at each

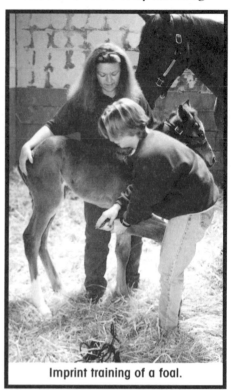

Imprint training of a foal.

body location until the foal shows signs of relaxation and submission. Further, the technique recommends presenting objects, handling, and other various stimuli specific to the expected career of the individual.

The "imprinting" assumption is that the early hours of a foal's life represent a special developmental stage, or critical period, for bonding to humans and for learning to tolerate all sorts of stimuli. In other words, the claim has been that this early handling will have greater lifelong positive effects on the horse's interaction with humans and its ability to learn than similar quality handling at any other time during the foal's development. The critical period assumption has not been proven; in fact, studies indicate that foals given such early handling, then left untended until reaching weanling or yearling age are no more or less accepting of humans or difficult to train.

Whether or not immediate neonatal handling is particularly effective, it is a convenient time to begin a handling program. The hour-old foal is typically much easier to capture and restrain than even a one-day old foal. This enables handling without an explosive episode that might instill fear. With daily calm and gentle handling, most foals do appear to learn to trust human handlers. While commercial marketing of the imprint training technique continues to stress the significance of handling during the early hours, Miller now recommends a long-term program of continued systematic daily handling similar to that recommended by good horse people for many decades.

One welfare concern with intensive early neonatal handling of foals is possible interference with bonding between the foal and the dam. I have known good veterinarians who have come to discourage their clients from early handling of foals. They have seen serious problems related to over-handling or of apparent disturbance of the mare-foal bond. Studies indicate that if the mare is calm and cooperative with your handling of the foal, mare-foal bonding is not likely to be disturbed.

Certain mares are highly protective of their foals, and attempts to handle the foal often are counterproductive in that the mare appears to communicate fear to the foal. Severe physical restraint, separation, or tranquilization of the mare for the sake of early handling of the foal would not be recommended. A gentle, common sense approach should avoid the "mauling" injuries that some veterinarians have attributed to early, intensive handling.

TRAINING IN THE ROUND PEN

The use of a round enclosure is a good, initial way to interact positively with an untrained horse. Round pen methods have been used for many decades, but have recently been popularized by a number of trainers who specialize in efficiently starting older unhandled horses. Working in a round pen is similar to working on a lunge line, but without the halter and line. Because the horse is safely contained and can still move forward at will, it allows the horse to learn some very important lessons about people even before submitting to handling, haltering, or leading. For previously unhandled animals, it allows for punishment-free communication by taking advantage of the horse's instinctual behavior. The horse's first reaction in the round

Training in the round pen.

pen is to escape from you. In the round pen, this results in running circles around you at the perimeter of the pen. The first step is to allow the horse to learn that all you want it to do is to stop running. By backing off from the horse each time it slows or stops, you can quickly train him to stop. The backing off is a form of negative reinforcement. A compromising trust is built on the basis that the horse can control your behavior as much as you are controlling his. This trust game forms the basis for closer work based on the horse's natural curiosity. "Now that you are a controllable threat, let's learn more about you." By walking away from the horse, the horse is encouraged to follow you. And then training can proceed very quickly.

There are many good books, tapes, and videos describing various interpretations of round pen or lunge line work. It's fun to compare and contrast the ideas and techniques of various specialists, and to adopt and develop your own protocols.

HORSE WHISPERERS

The term "horse whisperer" has its origin in the American West and refers to an individual who is particularly skilled at

Monty Roberts demonstrating his techniques.

handling horses and good at helping people better interact with their horses. The words "horse whisperer" imply a bit of mystique concerning extraordinary skills in understanding and communicating with horses. Horse whisperers are an earlier version of the guru super trainer who is willing to work with serious problem horses, particularly abused horses. They are typically known for quiet, methodical techniques based on observations of horses interacting with one another.

ANIMAL COMMUNICATORS AND PSYCHICS

The '90s terms "animal or horse communicator" or "psychic" refer to a person who claims the ability to read the mind of a horse, often from a distance, without ever having seen the horse. These individuals purport to operate in a number of modalities. They claim to be able to evaluate physical and mental health and illness by asking the horse. For example, a visiting veterinarian recently asked me if I thought a horse could tell someone (by mental telepathy) why it was not running at top speed, and more specifically that its amino acid balance was upset. One of this veterinarian's more progressive clients had consulted with an animal psychic who shared those results. Some psychics or communicators may genuinely believe that they can do these things, but in most instances the whole deal is a scam, pure and simple. Unless you can justify the costs as entertain-

Be skeptical of animal psychics.

ment or educational, please send your hard-earned dollars to a legitimate charity. Certainly don't delay veterinary evaluation and care of your horse or aggressively treat your horse on the basis of psychic advice.

CHAPTER 5

Common Behavior Problems and Behavior Modification

Horse behavior problems take many forms. Most are the result of learning failure. Many problems are the result of failure to become accustomed to natural fear and escape tendencies. Some are the result of failure to suppress a natural instinctive behavior that is incompatible with domestic behavior requirements. Some are failure to learn new, non-natural behaviors that most horses can learn. Others represent learning an undesirable behavior. Entire books and careers have been devoted to detailing horse behavior problems and suggested solutions. The following few examples represent the most common questions and cases concerning general behavior problems in our equine behavior clinic. These examples serve to illustrate concepts of behavior modification. The following two chapters address in more detail two broad classes of equine behavior problems — stereotypies and reproductive behavior problems.

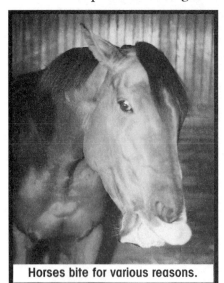

Horses bite for various reasons.

BITING

Horses bite for a number of different reasons. What you can do about it depends on the reason.

Biting and nipping are normal greeting behaviors for colts and stallions. This type of biting can be corrected quickly (within five minutes for most) simply by immediately smacking the horse on the lips with as much force as you can with your gloved hand, a small wand, or plastic bat. The secret is timing. If you can interrupt the head action as the bite is in progress, it takes even less time to break

> ## AT A GLANCE
>
> - Most behavior problems result from learning failure.
>
> - Effective punishment of unacceptable behavior such as biting must be swift.
>
> - Horses are easy to catch once they learn to associate you with positive things like food and water.
>
> - A calm, patient approach can accustom a horse to procedures it doesn't like, such as loading into a trailer.

the behavior. Horses in family groups stop biting with swift punishment. So that the horse doesn't become head shy, after the firm, well-timed smack on the lips, stay with the horse and reassure it with a gentle massage of the bridge of the nose.

Horses also bite in response to sharp pain. A horse which bites when in pain rarely develops a habit of biting, so once the pain is stopped, the biting stops.

Some horses become nippy after they have been fed treats from the hand. For horses which start to nip to get a treat, stop hand-feeding, and smack the lips as described for nipping and biting in colts and stallions. Be sure to be serious with the punishment. A little whack and a gentle "no-no-no" is often read by a horse as positive attention, and you will really be reinforcing rather than punishing the behavior.

Mares which have never offered to bite could do so when they have a new foal. They really are just being a good mom. So be careful around a new mom, she might do more than just bite you.

DIFFICULTY BEING CAUGHT

Otherwise well-trained horses which resist being caught, turn their butt on you in the stall, or run away from you in the pasture either are afraid of you or have not yet learned that you are a good thing and their life and well-being depends on you. They could fear you because they have just not overcome their instinctive fear of people and natural tendency to flee or because they have learned that you represent work and pain. They might not have learned that you are a good thing because no matter what they do, good or bad, they still receive good care.

The best way I know to cure catching difficulties reliably and rather permanently is to teach the horse that its food and water depend on you and being caught is always pleasant. It

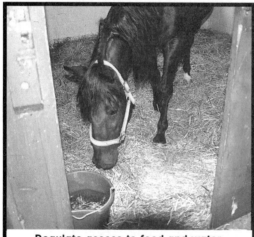

Regulate access to food and water.

might take about a week at most, but the lesson learned likely will last for the life of the horse. The horse needs to get very hungry and at least a little thirsty so that the association between you and feeding and watering is effectively made.

To do this, the horse has to be in a stall or paddock without lush grass and without continuous access to water, and you have to commit to all of its care for a week or so. To start out, hold all feed (hay and grain) for a day or more. Provide water twice daily at about 12-hour intervals in a bucket that you take to the stall. Stand quietly near the bucket until the horse approaches for a drink. If your horse doesn't approach the bucket, quietly reach down and trickle some water through your hands to ensure that it is clear this is water. If the horse doesn't drink after 10 minutes, step outside the stall door and sit on a bale of hay by the door for another 10 minutes. After the horse takes a drink, remove the bucket. Once the couple of days without feed have passed, start doing the same with a bucket that has a hand-full of grain, and offer a couple flakes of hay at the same time that you take the bucket of water.

Once your horse is reliably eating and drinking near you, you can start waiting until it lets you touch its halter before you actually give it the feed. If it is still shy or too quick at turning when you reach for its halter, an 18- to 24-inch length of catch rope attached to its halter can help you very quietly get a hand on it without a jerky rush to the halter. Gradually expect the horse to allow more and more contact before it gets the food reward. Gentle scratching at the withers similar to mutual grooming of horses is my favorite type of tactile contact with such a horse. Also introduce a simple command, such as "Come on," to associate with being caught and the reward.

After the horse is reliably approaching you head first and allowing contact at the stall door to get its food and water, try approaching it at other times throughout the day, sometimes with a small food treat and sometimes without. Then make the move to a larger area, until finally you can turn your horse out to pasture and it will come reliably to you. Remember your simple verbal command and the intermittent reinforcement with a treat. You might have to take your treat bucket with you at first.

HEAD SHYNESS

Head shyness is the term used to describe hyper-reactivity or hyper-sensitivity about the head. The sensitivity could be to the head in general or specific to the mouth, ears, or eyes. Rough handling, beating, or physical pain all can cause the problem. If there is no physical pain, it is an easy behavior to correct with patient, systematic desensitization. First, the horse should be handled in a kind and gentle manner to establish general trust. Specifically, grooming the horse is an excellent venue in which to gradually work your way back to handling the head.

VETERINARY PROCEDURE SHYNESS

Almost every horse I have ever known can learn to tolerate a little discomfort for a reward. The principles of teaching a horse to tolerate and sometimes even appear to enjoy a mildly uncomfortable procedure such as injection are simple:

• Begin by interacting with the horse in a way that produces a relaxed submissive posture. This can be grooming, stroking, or massaging at the neck.

• Avoid over-restraining. Often it is the tense manner and severe restraint that provokes resistance rather than the procedure itself.

• Maintain a calm and relaxed manner in conducting the procedure.

• Organize the situation so that a reaction on the part of the horse is least likely to cause a disturbance or hurt anyone. It is best if the horse can even move a bit and the technician can stay with the horse and continue the procedure. This teaches the horse that moving away doesn't change anything.

• Keep the procedure as painless as possible.

• Initially distract the horse with a salient reward during the procedure. For an injection this might be a small treat in a deep bucket.

• Give another reward immediately at the completion of the procedure.

It is best actually to devote time to training a horse for these procedures rather than to do them only when necessary. A few practice sessions made as realistic as possible will establish the confidence of both you and your horse, and make your veterinarian very happy. A fun project is to teach your horse some tricks on voice command. My favorite example is to teach a horse to raise its tail and relax its anus for temperature taking procedures. Start by gently and rhythmically massaging the head of the tail, then the anal area, which will cause a relaxation of the sphincter and a lifting of the tail. At approximately five second intervals during the massage, repeat a quiet, two-syllable voice command which will become a conditioned stimulus. I use "Lift tail," but you could use anything you wish. After about five repetitions, most horses will lift their tail and relax on voice command.

USE OF THE TWITCH

Some horses require restraint devices for breeding, veterinary procedures, and body clipping. A twitch applies pressure to the sensitive nerve endings in the nose. This inflicts pain, which initially distracts the horse from either noticing or responding to an unpleasant procedure. It usually particularly inhibits movement and kicking. That's why it is often used to restrain mares for breeding. The pain causes a release of natural analgesic chemicals in the brain, known as endogenous opiates or endorphins, which then likely mask both the pain at the nose and any discomfort elsewhere. You will see that after a few minutes the horse might get a droopy lip and drowsy, glazed-looking eyes. This drowsiness corresponds to high levels of endorphins in the blood. After about 10 to 15 minutes on the twitch, most horses become agitated. Some seem to explode or "blow the twitch." This period corresponds to lowering blood levels of endorphins, perhaps because the brain has temporarily depleted its supply.

A "humane" twitch.

Some horses seem to get to dislike the twitch, while others don't. This could be related to whether or not the twitch was removed during the relaxed drowsy (positive) state or whether they reached the obviously unpleasant point of "blowing the twitch."

LOADING INTO A TRAILER

Loading is probably the most common simple problem that horse owners face sooner or later. And this stands to reason. Entering a confined space that moves and rattles might be one of the least natural and counter instinctive activities we ask of horses. Most horses which don't load well are genuinely afraid. A few seem just stubborn.

The following tips may be useful in teaching your horse to load:

Avoid having to teach a horse how to load by trailering a young foal with its mom or a good traveler as early and often

Make sure the horse trusts you.

as practical during its early months. This takes advantage of the foal's natural drive to stay with its dam or the herd.

If you need to train a horse to load and travel, set aside a specific time for training, just as you would for starting a horse under saddle, or teaching it to jump.

Stay as calm and quiet as you can, and involve only those assistants who can also be calm and patient with the training process.

Start by making sure that the horse leads well and trusts you in other potentially fearful situations. The elements of loading that you can accustom your horse to separately before asking it to do it all at once are:

• following you on a ramp or bridge that gives a hollow sound

• following you from lighted to dark areas

• following you into a chute

• walking on a wheeled vehicle that rocks and gives with weight

Feeding your horse from a trailer is one sure way to make the trailer a positive environment. Some people train by placing an old trailer in the pasture and feeding grain from it, gradually advancing the feed bucket farther and farther forward. Once the horse is going all the way in for feed, you can practice leading the horse all the way in for its meals. You then can start feeding the horse some meals in your travel trailer outside the pasture and work up to actually going on practice trips.

Make the trailer as bright inside as possible. It often helps to have the a front door open to daylight.

Make the trailer as roomy looking as possible. Move the center partition if possible.

Avoid steep loading ramps.

A chute leading up to the ramp can make a big, positive difference for many horses.

A lunge rope running from the trailer on the off side of the horse and around the hindquarters between the hocks and the base of the tail to the handler or an assistant can effectively encourage and guide some horses which hesitate.

Load and unload calmly several times before taking the first trip. Then, make the ride as pleasant as possible.

Avoid punishment or trying to scare the horse into the trailer. In most instances, this only seems to assure the horse that the whole procedure is a bad deal.

Always reinforce the horse for entering with a treat of some sort and a word of praise.

HOW CAN I TELL WHETHER A PROBLEM IS A BEHAVIOR PROBLEM OR WHETHER IT INVOLVES SOMETHING PHYSICAL?

Sometimes it is not easy. Even when considering physical and mental problems in people who can talk, it is not easy to separate physical and behavioral primary and secondary components of behavior problems. In fairness to both you and your horse, a veterinarian should be consulted to consider any possible physical problems that might be the root cause or might be exacerbating a behavior problem, as well as to assist with any secondary physical problems resulting from a behavior problem. The ideal professional team for a behavior problem is an equine behavior specialist, the horse's general practice veterinarian, and any trainers, riders, or caretakers who are concerned.

Key questions for the team to consider include:

Could this be principally a behavior problem that has adverse effects on the physical health?

Is this principally a physical health problem causing a change in behavior?

Could this be a learned behavior?

How does the behavior vary with environment, season, work schedule, handler, diet?

There certainly are behavior problems that are simply behavior problems, but more often than not there is a primary or secondary physical component that should be addressed and monitored. For example, a young stallion which had nipped at the handler, was corrected, and now is head-shy might sound like a simple behavior problem. But the horse should be checked for any possible physical reason for head-shyness — ears, eyes, teeth, sinuses for example. Maybe the pain developed coincidentally with the punishment for biting. Maybe the horse was inadvertently injured by the punishment.

CAN HORSES PREFER PARTICULAR PEOPLE OR SEEM TO HATE OTHERS?

Yes, there is no question that horses recognize and can develop particular likes and dislikes for individuals. Their preferences and aversions also can generalize to a particular type of people — men, women, kids, short men, people who wear coveralls, smell like Nolvasan, and drive trucks with vet boxes.

It is also interesting to us in our studies of social behavior among domestic horses and wild equids that similar likes and dislikes for individual herd mates are apparent. We're also impressed with how long horses seem to remember individual people or herd mates, even after long periods of separation.

We once had two stallions living in a semi-feral bachelor herd, who seemed especially to dislike one another. James seemed to go out of his way to harass Jim. Jim would not readily submit, so they fought often. With other stallions, James was a relatively tolerant bachelor with ordinary sparring type interactions. One day James charged right through a fence to attack Jim. While fixing the fences and assessing for any injuries we separated the two by taking Jim to a distant enclosure. As it turned out he became involved in other work, so was not returned

Horses can develop likes and dislikes for certain individuals.

to the bachelor herd. Shortly thereafter he was sold to be a teaser stallion for a local breeding farm. Many years later the farm went bust and we took Jim back to live out his years in our semi-feral herd. Within the first minute of being turned out, James ran from a distant part of the enclosure, and this time broke through two fences to resume the battle with Jim. Jim won that battle. All who witnessed it were sure that James had remembered Jim and their relationship after the long absence. And we all were happy that we were not on James' @#$% list.

CHAPTER 6

Stereotypies

Cribbing, weaving, head shaking, self-mutilation, and other stereotypies are the most common and frustrating behavior problems of horses. In some countries they are considered a serious unsoundness.

WHAT ARE STEREOTYPIES?

Stereotypies are repetitive, highly stylized, seemingly functionless motor responses and sequences. They occur in all captive wild and domestic species. The classic equine stereotypies are listed in the chart on the next page. The usual classification includes locomotor behaviors, oral behaviors, and a special class of self-mutilative behaviors. In addition to these classic stereotypies, horses can develop a wide variety of other repetitive movements, such as banging a bucket or jiggling a door, that would be classified at stereotypical.

HOW COMMON ARE STEREOTYPIES?

Estimates of the prevalence of stereotypies among domestic horses have ranged considerably, from as low as 1% to as high as 25%. The incidence varies among subpopulations of horses. Some particular establishments have a relatively stereotypy-free population, while others can be found to have very high incidence. Certain environments, such as racetrack stables, have a reputation of having a high incidence of stereotypies. The incidence of stereotypies is much higher in captive wild equids, such as Przewalski horses or zebras stabled in zoos. Similarly, the severity of a stereotypy varies considerably among horses and within an individual over time.

EQUINE STEREOTYPIES

ORAL	LOCOMOTOR	SELF-MUTILATION
cribbing, tongue movements, lip movements	head movements (bobbing, tossing, shaking, swinging, nodding), throat rubbing, pacing, weaving, fence or stall walking, circling, stomping, kicking, pawing, digging	self-biting (flank, chest, shoulder), wall-kicking, lunging into objects.

WHY DO HORSE DO THESE THINGS?

Stereotypies remain one of most perplexing behavior problems. It is not clear whether stereotypies should be viewed as abnormal behavior, misbehavior, or whether they represent a normal "coping" behavior in response to stress or pain. Probably most animal owners, veterinarians, and behaviorists would agree that we should strive to prevent stereotypies from developing by preventing or eliminating any discomfort that would provoke the behavior initially and by providing low-stress environments. Where there may be more disagreement is what should be done should stereotypies develop.

There also remains considerable controversy about the factors involved in stereotypies in horses as well as in other species. Management conditions (housing, social, exercise, nutrition) and genetic predisposition are considered important factors. A consistent observation is that some horses appear much more likely to perform a stereotypy than others, so appear predisposed to one or more stereotypies.

There is also suggestion that the predisposition could run in families. Behavioral scientists from Scotland recently surveyed the history of stereotypies among captive Przewalski horses for which breeding histories are well documented. They concluded that genetics is an important predisposing factor.

The view that all stereotypies are abnormal and the result of boredom or frustration of stable life is now known to be too narrow. Certainly there can be medical causes, yet for a large percentage of the cases one cannot be identified. In many of these the behavior might appear genuine, as opposed to a simple attention getting or "boredom" activity. In some individuals, no matter what the root cause, the stereotypy clearly appears exacerbated by social, nutrition, and exercise factors.

For most stereotypies, we should probably never stop looking for a possible physical cause. A great example illustrating this point is the case of head shaking. For many years, veterinarians have looked and looked for possible sources of discomfort in cases of head shaking. Scientists in the United Kingdom and California just recently have found that some head shaking in horses appears to be induced by bright light. The syndrome has been called photic head shaking. It is similar to the photic sneeze syndrome in humans, which occurs in some fair-haired, blue-eyed people. With changes from dark to bright light, they experience uncontrollable sneezing episodes. It is known that the sneezing results from a hyperactivation of the trigeminal nerve in response to bright light. In humans, this syndrome is now known to be genetic. The bright light-induced head shake in the horse is a more violent and irregular, snorting toss of the head, compared to the more rhythmic traditional head bobbing or nodding seen as a classic stereotypy. The horse might appear to be trying to scratch its nose on a foreleg or on the ground as it snorts. This can become dangerous as the horse will try to scratch its nose even working at a trot or canter. Photic head shaking almost always worsens under work, and immediately subsides as the animal is returned to the barn or rest. So it can be easily misinterpreted as a purely behavior problem. In most cases, photic head shaking is seasonal, and will quiet immediately when the eyes are covered or the area is darkened. These horses tend to seek shade. Dark goggles or sun-blocking face masks could be all that is needed to relieve most of the head shaking for some of these horses. Also, the head shaking often subsides if the horse is treated with cyproheptadine, a medication that effectively can block the reaction physiologically. Within the

Masks can help some head shakers.

last two years it has been found that light sensitive horses are also often sensitive in the same way to sharp, loud noises.

Several laboratories have confirmed that endogenous opiates (endorphins) rise during the performance of a stereotypy in horses. In horses which perform a stereotypy in the absence of an identifiable physical, medical, or apparent environmental cause, the assumption is made that the behavior likely initially had a tangible cause, but has now become a habit maintained by the reward of opiate release.

The trend in clinical veterinary behavior has been to call stereotypies "obsessive-compulsive disorder," or OCD. This syndrome, first identified in humans, has two components. One component is the compulsive, repetitive behavior, such as repeatedly checking to see if the stove has been left on. The other component is the accompanying obsessive thoughts or worries, such as concerns about being caught in a burning building. Often the thoughts or worries are related to the compulsive behavior and logically appear to drive it. In the case of animals we do not know whether they think or worry, so this label might be too elaborate. Weaving or cribbing in a horse might not involve any specific worry or thought, and could be more like toe-tapping or nail biting stereotypies in humans.

WHAT CAN OR SHOULD BE DONE?

Treatment of equine stereotypies is now a controversial topic. First of all, there are very few effective treatments. Also, we must consider that if a stereotypy is a normal behavioral mechanism for coping with stress, should we try to treat it in any way other than eliminating the stressful cause? Anti-cribbing surgery, aversive conditioning, physical restraint, and pharmacological treatments are now being seriously questioned.

Usually it is difficult to identify and/or eliminate the particular stressful aspects of the domestic environment responsible for a particular stereotypy. Nonetheless, most horse owners and managers would like to try to reduce or eliminate such behavior. Changes in management that are most likely to result in reduced stereotypy include physical and social environmental manipulation and nutritional changes in the direction of more roughage and less concentrated feeds. Systematic behavior evaluation, including detailed study of 24-hour videotaped samples of the horse's behavior, usually can provide clues about the possible causes and exacerbating factors that can guide an individualized management and treatment program. For example, there are certain horses which do their stereotypy only when people are present in the barn. In such cases, people are not there most of the time, so the majority of the animal's 24-hour time budget looks normal. The owners often decide not to pursue treatment, even though they are not happy that they appear to provoke the problem behavior.

A large percentage of the effort, thought, and certainly expense of treatment of weaving, pacing, cribbing, self-mutilation, and other stereotypies in horses has involved various methods of physically preventing or discouraging the behavior. Physical restraint sometimes helps, but rarely cures these problems. When the horse is effectively restrained from performing one behavior, all too often another problem behavior develops. For locomotor stereotypies, such as weaving, pacing, or circling, probably the most effective management changes are more social contact, and a diet with as little grain and as much grass or grass hay as possible. For a stallion, most stereotypies can be relieved significantly if the stallion is turned out in a large pasture with one or more mares to care for. In this situation, the stallion becomes a harem stallion with great responsibility to herd and defend the mares. Those harem maintenance behaviors seem to occupy the stallion's time and distract him from his stereotypy. Of course, this is not often a plausible solution. There might be some difficulty and danger in taking such a stallion or his mares in and out of such a situation. Most stallions will not want to leave their mares.

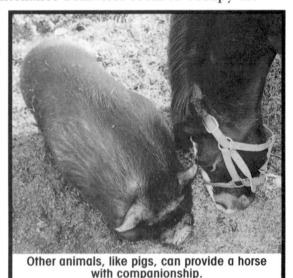

Other animals, like pigs, can provide a horse with companionship.

Horses appear to find meaningful social companionship from animals of other species. Donkey, goat, rabbit, and even chicken stall companions are sometimes useful in relieving stereotypies in horses. In my experience, horses with chickens as stall companions sometimes stop moving about in an effort keep the chicken calm, or in an effort not to step on the chicken.

Aversive conditioning (or punishment) of the stereotypy is rarely effective. It is common for people to yell at their horses, and this also rarely has much of an effect. Some horses actually learn to do these things for attention. Pawing, in particular, can be taught to just about any horse by first provoking the behavior, then yelling at the horse each time it does it. You can demonstrate this with just about any horse. Just tie it up about three feet short of a bucket of grain, which almost always provokes pawing. Yell at the horse each time it paws; the rate of pawing will increase. If you ignore the pawing, it rapidly subsides. You probably don't want to do this, but if you were to repeat the procedure a few times, you are likely to get a horse that paws each time you tie it, or maybe each time you see it or yell at it.

Pharmacological aids which in some cases have appeared helpful include long-acting tranquilizers, tricyclic anti-depressants, and l-tryptophan supplementation.

Acupuncture and acupressure methods are under development for treatment of behavior problems in horses. Auriculotherapy in the form of acupuncture, acupressure, or surgical stapling of the ears is currently popular in some regions of the country. The same procedures used to relieve estrus cycle and ovarian problems are used for stereotypies. Unfortunately, the efficacy of these methods is still questionable.

CRIBBERS DON'T SWALLOW THE AIR

Workers in the United Kingdom have studied the mechanics of cribbing by using endoscopy and fluoroscopy. Their findings indicate that during cribbing, air is not actually swallowed into the stomach. Rather a bolus of air is formed in the esophagus, then expelled. The characteristic grunt occurs as incoming air enters the throat. Actually, if you watch careful-

A foal "champing" in submission to a stallion (above); the foal below has mistakenly tried to nurse from a stallion, which is giving only a mild warning.

A stallion approaching a mare which is showing estrus (above);
and proceeding with a pasture breeding (below).

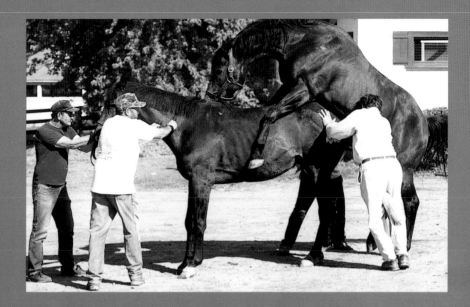

Two ways of managed breeding: with moderate assistance and occurring outside (above), and in the breeding shed with a team of handlers and a mare with a breeding shield and twitch.

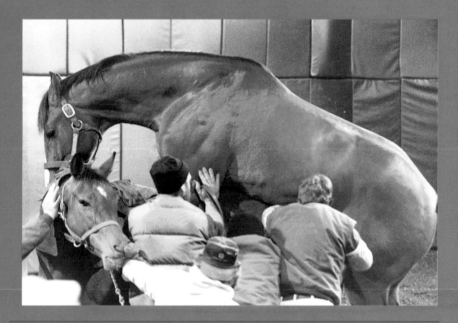

A herd of bachelor stallions living harmoniously (above); a harem
stallion herding his mares (below).

Under natural conditions, weaning is a long, gradual process, as shown by this foal's 2-year-old dam (above) nursing its own dam; (below) domestic horses usually are weaned abruptly by six months.

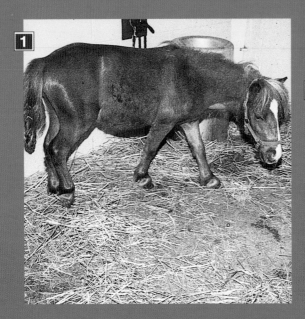

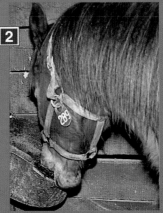

Examples of stereotypies: 1) Stall circling; 2) Cribbing (note the association with feed); 3) Pawing.

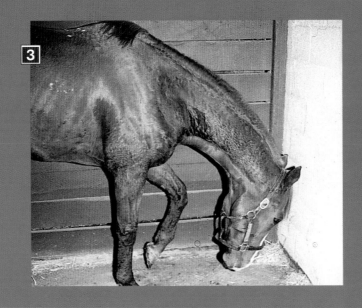

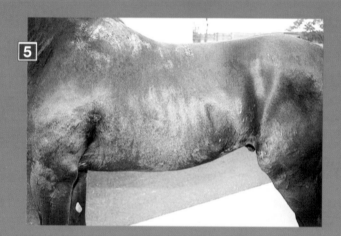

4) Fence walking; 5) Self-mutilation;
6) A muzzle to reduce injury from self-
mutilation.

1) A pony reacting to an anticipated injection; 2 & 3) becoming calm and increasingly submissive; 4) getting rewarded for standing quietly for the injection.

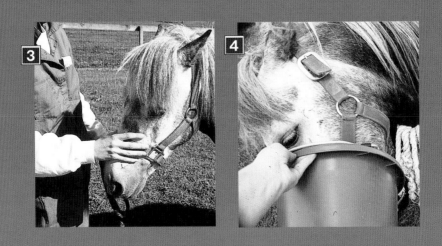

ly while a horse is cribbing you can see for yourself that the bolus does not appear to be swallowed beyond the throat. The belief that many cribbers colic because of the swallowed air has to be rethought in light of this finding. One explanation for

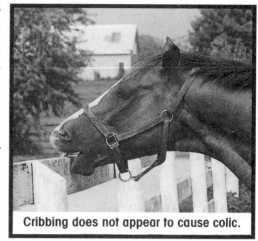

Cribbing does not appear to cause colic.

the perceived association of colic with cribbing might be that something else is causing both. Another is that some exceptional horses might swallow air.

CHAPTER 7

Reproductive Behavior Problems

Domestic horses in general are quite cooperative and successful with hand breeding. However, they do have some common problems, many of which can be avoided or corrected with simple management changes.

BREEDING STALLIONS

Sexual Interest and Arousal (Libido) Problems

Specific stallion libido problems include slow starting novices, slow or sour experienced stallions, and specific aversions or preferences. The majority of these problems are entirely or partly manmade. Most respond well to behavior therapy alone or in combination with medication that overrides the effects of bad experiences which might have created the problem in the first place. Some cases are hormone-related and can improve with management aimed at increasing exposure to mares and reduced exposure to other stallions. Typically, this will increase reproductive hormone levels, sexual interest, and arousal.

Specific Erection and Ejaculation Dysfunction

Libido-independent erection dysfunction is rare in stallions. In contrast, ejaculation dysfunction is a relatively common problem which can be related to libido, experience, pain, specific dysfunction of the ejaculatory apparatus, and genital tract pathology. There are a variety of management changes and pharmacological aids that can improve ejaculation function.

Rowdy Breeding Stallions

Rowdy misbehavior in breeding stallions also is largely manmade. Most problems can be overcome with judicious, skillful, respectful training. As with dogs, it is the rare exception that even the most misbehaved, mishandled stallion cannot become retrained in a matter of less than one or two hours. As with pet training, stallion handlers typically need more actual training time than the stallion. Veterinarians can help their clients and patients by understanding and conveying to their clients the basic behavioral expectations of a hand-bred stallion, principles of training a breeding stallion, and where to find professional help in training or retraining a breeding stallion.

Stallions can be retrained.

Combining Breeding and Performing

Opinions vary among owners and trainers concerning whether stallions should combine breeding and performance careers. Some people strongly believe that a stallion will lose interest in performance and/or become more difficult to handle once he has had breeding experience. Some trainers believe that the physical demands of mounting and breeding can adversely affect high level dressage or jumping performance, and some breeding farm managers believe that performance demands will limit a stallion's fertility. Others believe that stallions become more poised and manageable, both for breeding and performance, when the two careers are combined. None of these beliefs has been scientifically tested. Factors affecting the outcome for a particular stallion include individual stallion variation, the level and demands of each career, and most importantly the organization, attitudes, and expectations of owners, trainers, and breeding managers.

MASTURBATION

Free-running and pastured stallions, regardless of age (newborn to aged), sociosexual environment, bachelor or harem status, or species (zebra, donkeys, Przewalski horses, or horses), exhibit periodic spontaneous erections and penile movements at the rate of about one three-minute episode every 90 minutes. Ejaculation is rare. The rate is the same for domestic stallions regardless of breed, type of housing, type and level of work, sociosexual environment, breeding status, androgen levels, libido, or fertility. Similar periodic erections are common to all mammals studied, including humans. This phenomenon appears to be normal, healthy, and necessary.

A considerable portion of the horse breeding and performing industries still view spontaneous erection and penile movements as inappropriate or abnormal behavior that should be eliminated. Anti-masturbatory devices for stallions are still widely used. Unfortunately, stallion rings, cages, spike pads, and brushes can be easily acquired from saddle shops and horsemen's mail order catalogs. In 1995, a shock collar device recommended for stopping masturbation in stallions was released from a Colorado manufacturer and widely marketed internationally.

Our observations indicate that anti-masturbatory devices rarely reduce spontaneous erection and penile movements. Our greatest concern about spontaneous erection and masturbation is the physical injury and secondary psychological harm to stallions by such attempts to stop the behavior. A high percentage of stallions which develop libido, erection, and/or ejaculation dysfunction, have physical scars from anti-masturbatory devices, with behavior suggesting particular fear of punishment for erection.

BROODMARES

Mares normally show estrus and ovulate during spring and summer months, known as the breeding season. Some continue to ovulate and show estrus through the fall and winter as well. Ovulation occurs approximately every 21 days, and estrus lasts about three to four days before ovulation and can continue for one or two days after ovulation. The main elements of estrus behavior in the mare are: approaching the stallion, tolerating teasing by the stallion, presenting the hind quarters to the stallion, lifting the tail up and to the side, frequent urination, turning the head back in a relaxed fashion, and flexing a foreleg.

A mare in estrus tolerates teasing.

The two most common problems associated with estrus in breeding mares are failure to show estrus and failure to stand for hand breeding.

Failure to show estrus

A common complaint is that certain mares fail to show estrus. While there are rare conditions in which mares are not ovulating and showing estrus, in most cases they are cycling normally and careful teasing will reveal subtle, but detectable signs. The majority of these cycling mares will "break down" after prolonged or creative teasing. In some cases, a difficult mare will signal estrus more readily if she is teased in an unrestrained, as opposed to haltered, situation. For example, a mare which does not show typical estrus with conventional in hand or stall teasing could reliably signal estrus if placed in a paddock with the stallion presented at the fence line or pastured in a neighboring paddock. This situation expands the possible behavioral signals of estrus to some of the more subtle, yet reliable indicators of sexual interest in the stallion. Although the mare might not actually break down, she might under these conditions reliably approach the stallion when close to ovulation. The type of teasing required for some mares could represent considerable extra time and effort which is simply not practical in most situations. It might be more efficient to have these mares examined regularly by a veterinarian using ultrasound to determine readiness to breed. One explanation for failure to show estrus among mares with normal ovaries is exposure to steroids. For example, recently retired racing or performance mares which have been given androgenic anabolic steroids often do not show normal estrus, even when the ovaries appear to be undergoing normal cyclic changes. Failure to show estrus also can occur in mares in early stages of androgen-secreting ovarian tumors.

Failure to stand for breeding

Some mares show estrus when teased but refuse to stand for in-hand breeding. They appear anxious as the stallion approaches for breeding, often dangerously "exploding" when the stallion mounts. Many such mares reportedly become worse when more severe restraint is applied. Observations of free-running wild and domestic horses suggest that under natural field breeding conditions, mares might show mild estrus for many days before actual breeding occurs. Stallions might mount many times during this period, as though testing the receptivity of the mare. Mares sometimes walk away from the stallion as he mounts. In the domestic situation, it is reasonable to expect that many of the explosive reactions of mares during hand breeding result from or are aggravated by management factors, including improper time for breeding, inadequate socialization of the mare during development, or fear induced by restraint during breeding. In some cases this behavior seems complicated by a mare's apparent worry over her foal at her side or separated during breeding.

Although rare, sometimes a mare can show estrus during pregnancy. The estrus might be mild and intermittent.

PERFORMANCE MARES

One of the most common complaints of owners and riders of performance mares involves reproductive behavior. One involves the mare which shows very intense estrus. For unknown reasons, mares vary considerably in the intensity of estrus. For example, some mares only show estrus when actively teased by a stallion. Others reliably show estrus in response to other mares or even to people. These mares, although usually the breeding farm manager's delight, can be a problem during training or performance. Some

Some performance mares show little estrus.

of these mares have been known to stop, lift their tail, urinate, and present their hind quarters to any gelding or stallion encountered at a show or event. Most mares can be controlled under show or performance conditions, but extreme cases will show estrus even under saddle. Treatment with progestogens can effectively suppress estrus.

Often, cases of estrus behavior that generate complaints are not actually estrus behavior, but when examined carefully, similar behavior misinterpreted as estrus. Some mares exhibit a submissive cowering and urine squirting behavioral sequence, which is easily mistaken for estrus. Some racehorse trainers call this "starting gate estrus." If such mares are teased daily with a stallion through one or more estrus cycles, their "true" estrus, distinct from their submissive behavior, usually can be detected. Clitoral wink, tail raise, full urination, and breeding posture are usually not elements of the submissive behavior. Another distinguishing aspect is that submissive cowering and urination can be elicited by any threatening situation, while estrous posture and urination usually are more pronounced in response to a stallion. Frequent urination, tail lifting, and straining associated with uro-vaginal irritation also can be easily mistaken for estrus. One of the most interesting cases was a mare thought to be showing estrus whenever under saddle. She would stop, lift her tail, and strain. Careful examination by a reproduction veterinarian revealed that this mare had a sliver of a tree branch impaled in her vagina, with resulting inflammation and infection. As expected, the behavior problem resolved once the foreign object and infection were eliminated.

ESTRUS CYCLE-RELATED PERFORMANCE PROBLEMS

A relatively common problem behavior reported by trainers and riders of mares is variable performance or "trainability" related to the estrus cycle. The most common interpretation is that the mare becomes less cooperative or attentive to the performance tasks during estrus. During work, the mare might actually be distracted by or show estrus to stallions, geldings, or even other mares. Careful clinical evaluation has confirmed that some mares do show periods of deterioration, either mild or marked, of performance or temperament associated with a particular stage of the ovarian cycle. Similarly, some mares are simply hyperexcitable and generally difficult to handle at certain stages of the cycle. Some mares appear particularly sensitive to weight or manipulation that might affect the area of the ovaries during the periovulatory period of the cycle. The problem behavior is not always associated with estrus or ovulation. In some cases, the mare's best behavior might be during estrus and the problem behavior is associated with the diestrus phase of the cycle.

Evaluation of estrus cycle-related problems can be complicated. Performance or training problems are part of a complex array of human-animal interactions that are difficult to evaluate objectively. Like many behavior problems, the historical details of the problem's emergence and attempts at various corrective measures are often especially difficult to establish among owners,

Behavior can change during estrus.

trainers, and caretakers involved. However, in several cases we have evaluated systematically sexual behavior, performance behavior, general handling behavior, ovarian activity, and steroid hormones over two or more cycles. During the period of study, the persons evaluating each aspect remained "blind" to each other's results. Such evaluations have confirmed that in some cases day-to-day changes in temperament, trainability, performance, and tractability can occur in association with certain periods of apparently normal ovarian cycles and estrous periods. In many other cases, an association with the estrus cycle is confidently ruled out by such a detailed evaluation, in which case other causes for the intermittent behavior problems can be explored.

The underlying reasons for cycle-related performance problems are far from fully understood at this time. Accordingly, therapeutic recommendations are limited. After careful observation of the problem behavior, as well as endocrine and physical examination to rule out a pathological condition requiring attention, one might consider progesterone therapy for those mares whose problems are associated with estrus. Progesterone at certain dose levels will suppress ovarian cycling, leaving the mare with low levels of estrogen and high levels of progesterone. Either progesterone in oil or any of several synthetic progestin preparations can be tried. There seems to be considerable individual mare variation in the behavioral response to different products and doses. Many mares appear to have a positive response to progesterone therapy even at levels that do not suppress the ovarian cycle. Hormone implants developed for use in the cattle industry have been used regionally over the past few years, as has long-acting injectable progesterone. Current research indicates that at the usual doses these treatments do not actually suppress ovarian function and estrus in response to teasing by a stallion. Nonetheless, riders and trainers often report improved performance behavior during treatment.

A commonly asked question is whether mares with cycle-related behavior problems might improve if the mare were to be pregnant, a natural state of high progesterone. Again, there has been no reported research on this question, only anecdotes that many mares which have had these types of behavior problems do seem to mellow to a reasonably good and consistent performance during pregnancy.

For mares whose problem behavior is associated with diestrus, repeated short-cycling with prostaglandin might be useful. Long-acting tranquilization regimens also have proven useful in a number of recent cases, with the reported positive effect of a general mellowing of the mare.

SPAYING MARES

If there are behavior problems that seem to be associated with the ovarian cycle of a mare which you don't plan to breed, then why not remove the ovaries? In a limited number of instances this might be helpful. The first question to ask when considering spaying is, "How is this mare during the winter?" For most mares, the ovaries stop functioning (anestrus) during the winter. So hormonally, an anestrous mare is in a state similar to having been spayed, principally low estrogen and low progesterone. Of course, many other training and environmental factors that affect behavior and obviously vary systematically with seasons might confound your interpretations. Another unusual phenomenon in the mare should be clearly understood before considering spaying. In most species other than horses, low progesterone and high estrogen are required to induce estrus behavior in the female. So in those species, removal of the ovaries removes estrogen, and there is no estrous behavior. In the mare, however, all that is needed for display of estrous behavior is low progesterone. The addition of estrogen usually intensifies estrous behavior, but it is not needed. So the spayed mare which has no progesterone typically will show estrus, at least at a low level, at any time. Spaying could make matters worse if the mare's performance problems truly have been associated with estrus.

STALLION-LIKE BEHAVIOR IN MARES

Male sexual behavior responses are not a normal aspect of mare behavior. For example, while it is normal for cows to mount other cows, and jennets to mount other jennets, it is unusual for horse mares to mount one another. Any persistent male-typical behavior (posture and gait, vocalization pattern, herding, teasing, elimination-marking behavior, copulatory responses, inter-male aggression) in a mare should be viewed as abnormal. Such behavior suggests the presence, at one time or another, of abnormally high androgen levels. The two most common sources of androgen associated with stallion-like behavior in mares are steroid hormones given to the mare (testosterone, estrogen, or androgenic anabolic steroids) and ovarian tumors that can produce high levels of any of the steroid hormones. Stallion-like behavior often persists for weeks to months after the source of androgen is removed and measurable circulating androgens return to normal mare levels. However, the intensity of male-type behavior usually subsides within a few weeks after removal of androgen.

In some cases, stallion-like behavior is observed during pregnancy. Owners often find male-type behavior especially disturbing in pregnant mares. Such mares might actively herd and mount other mares, which raises concerns for all of the pregnant mares. If the stallion-like mare is separated from other mares, she could run fence lines or otherwise become disturbed by mares just as stallions do. Currently, there are two possible explanations for the emergence of stallion-like behavior in pregnant mares. Granulosa cell tumors on the ovary can become evident coincident with pregnancy. Depending on the tumor's size and the stage of pregnancy, these can be removed during pregnancy or after parturition. Secondly, the fetal-placental unit does produce steroids during pregnancy. These usually do not affect mare behavior, but could in some cases. There certainly are mares which continue to show stallion-like behavior through pregnancy, then stop soon after parturition, and in which no tumor is ever identified.

MATERNAL BEHAVIOR PROBLEMS

Inadequate or abnormal mothering behavior of mares is a relatively rare, yet urgent problem. The causes of poor maternal behavior as well as the most efficient course of intervention or therapy for the various types of problems are controversial. In general, problems are more common among first-time mothers, and often recur in the same mare. The abnormal behavior usually occurs immediately after parturition, but in some cases can emerge after one or several days of normal behavior. The urgent task is to determine the specific nature of the problem while maintaining the safety and strength of the foal and the potential for maintaining the bond.

There are at least six distinct categories of inadequate or aberrant maternal behavior in mares:

Ambivalence. The absence of attention to a foal, bonding behavior, and protective behavior is most commonly found with sick, weak, or medicated mares and/or foals, or in mares and foals separated or over-manipulated during the periparturient period. Normal maternal-foal interaction should commence as the strength of one or the other returns. In cases where a decision is made to try to revive the bond, it is best to keep the animals together with minimal disturbance necessary for supportive health care.

Extreme protectiveness. Another problem involves excessive aggression toward humans or other animals, seemingly related to extreme protectiveness of the foal. While strong maternal protectiveness in free-running conditions might be celebrated, in the domestic situation it actually can lead to injury of the foal. While rushing to interpose herself between the foal and a perceived threat, the mare could trample or push the foal into manmade obstacles in confined conditions. The intensity of such protectiveness typically subsides within a few days but in some

Some mares are extremely protective of their foals.

mares could persist through weaning. Efforts to avoid making the mare feel protective when the foal is in a position where it might be trampled, coupled with deliberate training of the mare to accept necessary intruders, usually are adequate solutions. Injuries to the young foal might be less likely in a large stall or paddock, than if in a small stall. Even when directly witnessed, protective behavior easily can be misinterpreted as an attack of the foal. In open spaces, these mares rarely injure the foal, so diagnosis would be facilitated by moving from a stall to a large paddock.

Fear of the foal. Some mares, usually young, first-time mothers, appear to be afraid of their foal. In such mares, normal bonding and protective behavior are not present. Instead the mare tries to get away from the foal. Some of these mares appear to acclimate rather quickly to the presence of the foal, as they would to any novel object or animal but continue to avoid or escape the foal if it tries to nurse.

Nursing avoidance. This typically, but not always, occurs with obvious udder edema and sensitivity to tactile stimulation. Positive bonding behavior and protectiveness can remain normal. For nursing avoidance or mild aggression, nursing supervision with physical restraint of the mare under halter and/or in a nursing chute can be helpful.

True foal rejection. Savage attack of a foal by its dam is relatively rare, but usually life threatening to the foal. The most urgent problem is savage offensive attack, with lowered head and opened mouth biting or grasping the withers, neck, or back of the foal. The dam may lift, shake, and toss the foal against an object, or stamp and hold it to the ground. In contrast to foals injured by over-protective mares, fearful mares, or mares resisting nursing, savagely attacked foals usually have bite wounds and serious multiple skeletal injuries. The only recommended practical long-term solution is permanent separation of the mare and foal. Savage attack often follows one or more days of apparently normal acceptance, bonding behavior, protection, and nursing of the foal, and it usually repeats if the mare and foal are not separated. It is for this reason that supervision, restraint, or tranquilization are rarely practical solutions. Savage attack of foals usually repeats with subsequent foals.

Foal stealing. A rare, but interesting maternal behavior problem is the adoption or stealing of the foals of other mares. The stealing usually occurs within a day or two before the "thief" mare gives birth to her own foal. When she has her own foal, she usually abandons the stolen foal. The stolen foal might not be re-accepted by its original dam.

ORPHAN FOALS

Hand-feeding in isolation from other foals or horses often results in behavioral maladjustments of the foal as it matures. The hand-fed foal often appears to become bonded socially to humans rather than to horses. This might be satisfying to the caretaker initially, but can quickly become dangerous. The most common complaint is that hand-fed foals tend to lose their fear and respect of humans, so they "walk all over" human handlers. The hand-reared foal might try to initiate play or sexual behavior with humans. One good solution for raising an orphan is to immediately place it with a lactating foster mare,

A foal "kindergarten."

known as a nurse mare. These are mares which might have lost their own foal, or have an older foal which can be weaned. If an orphan foal must be bucket or bottle fed, the usual recommendation is to keep the foal with other horses and minimize contact with humans. Some farms offer the service of raising groups of orphan foals together. These are known as kindergartens. To promote normal socialization, the foals are tub-fed together with minimal human contact. An interesting feature is that older foals often seem to "mother" newly added young foals.

CHAPTER 8

Professional Equine Behaviorists

A variety of professionals understand horse behavior and problems. Some of the best equine behaviorists are amateur and professional horse trainers with extraordinary skills and experience. Unfortunately, there is no organization or certification of expert horse trainers that can ensure good credentials.

At present there are two organizations which offer professional certification in the area of clinical animal behavior consulting. These are the Animal Behavior Society (ABS) and the American Veterinary Medical Association (AVMA).

The Animal Behavior Society is a scientific and professional organization of animal behaviorists trained in a variety of biobehavioral disciplines, including zoology, psychology, animal science, and veterinary medicine. In 1991, the ABS board of professional certification began certifying practitioners of applied animal behavior. This certification process ensures minimum education, experiential, and ethical standards for the professional applied animal behavior practitioner. Two levels of professional certification can be achieved. Applied Animal Behaviorist Certification requires either 1) a doctoral degree in a biological or behavioral science with an emphasis on animal behavior and a minimum of particular courses plus five years of professional experience in applied animal behavior, or 2) a doctorate in veterinary medicine plus a two-year approved residency program in animal behavior. Associate Applied Animal Behaviorist Certification requires training at the master's level or a comparable minimum of graduate courses in animal behavior plus two years of professional experience in applied animal behavior. Although certification is not by animal species, individuals usually specialize in a limited number of species. There are currently about 30 certified applied animal behaviorists in North America, only a few of whom specialize in equine behavior. Further information and a list of Certified Applied Animal Behaviorists can be found on the ABS World Wide Web site (the site address changes with changing leadership, so search "Animal Behavior Society.")

In 1993, the American Veterinary Medical Association recognized the specialty of animal behavior practice, forming the American College of Veterinary Behaviorists. Board certification requires a doctorate in veterinary medicine and a clinical residency or comparable experience followed by a formal examination procedure. Veterinary behaviorists are not certified by species, but of the 20 current diplomates, about half specialize in small pet animal practice, and about half include horses in their practice. Further information and a list of ACVB Diplomates can be found on the AVMA web site at www.AVMA.org.

Do mares get PMS?

Well, the short answer is no, because they don't have a menstrual cycle like primates. So they can't get pre-menstrual syndrome. But the correct answer is that mares can have changes in temperament and performance related to their ovarian cycle. Among mares, it is not always at the time of the cycle that would correspond to the premenstrual time in primates. See Chapter 7 for details.

Does Viagra work in horses?

Viagra and other similar compounds enhance an erection by facilitating vasodilation of the spongy tissues of the penis. These drugs don't directly improve sex drive, just the quality of the erection. In people, there are lots of medical conditions, such as diabetes and cardiovascular conditions, as well as medications, that reduce the rigidity of erection. Inadequate erection independent of a libido problem is rare in stallions. Once a stallion gets aroused, erection is usually normal. So even though Viagra and similar drugs would likely work on a stallion that had an erection problem, there is not much call for it.

Anthropomorphic — Attributing human characteristics, particularly emotion and motivation, to animals.

Aversive conditioning — Use of aversive stimuli in the form of negative reinforcement or punishment to modify behavior.

Cognitive ability or cognition — Higher mental processes such as mental imaging, rational thinking, problem solving, or mental modeling that cannot be directly observed but are inferred from behavior.

Champing, snapping — The characteristic submissive response of young equids which includes a lowering of the head and mouth movements similar to exaggerated sucking.

Classical conditioning — Pairing of an unconditioned stimulus (tug back on the lead shank) with a conditioned stimulus (whoa) so that the conditioned stimulus evokes the unconditioned response stop.

Counter-conditioning — Replacement of a particular undesirable response with a neutral or desirable response that is incompatible with the undesirable response.

Critical period — A period during development when the individual is optimally ready to learn certain response patterns.

Elimination-marking behaviors — Characteristic behavioral sequences in response to urination and defecation. In stallions, elimination marking includes particular attention to any urine or feces, sniffing, flehmen response, and covering with urine or feces.

Estrus — Behavior characteristic of the sexually receptive state.

Flehmen — An olfactory-related response of animals in response to pungent odors involving a raising of the nose, curling of the lip, and drawing of air and fluids into the vomeronasal ducts.

Flooding — A concept of behavior modification involving desensitization by overwhelming the individual with stimulation.

Gentling — A term used for interacting with horses in a calm and quiet manner using mostly positive reinforcement or gentle negative reinforcement to modify behavior.

Habituation — A simple form of learning involving reduction in an unlearned response to a stimulus with repeated occurrence of the stimulus.

Horse (or animal) communicator — An individual claiming ability to communicate telepathically with animals.

Horse whisperer — A term used in North America for an individual with extraordinary experience-based abilities in communicating and training horses.

Human-bonded — A condition in which a non-human animal responds to a human as it would to its own species. This may include sexual response.

Imprinting — A term used by ethologists for a species-specific type of learning that occurs within a limited period early in life (critical period), in which the animal "permanently bonds" to something in its environment, usually its first caregiver. Classic examples are ducklings that instinctively follow the first moving object in their environment (usually their mother).

Insight learning — Behavior modification or problem solving as a result of thinking or "mental modeling," as opposed to experience-based learning.

Learning — A specific change or modification of behavior as a result of experience with an external event or series of events.

Mutual grooming — Two individuals simultaneously grooming one another.

Negative reinforcement — An aversive stimulus that is removed contingent upon a response.

Operant conditioning (also known as instrumental conditioning) — The strengthening or weakening of a response depending on the consequences.

Pheromone — A specific chemical secreted as a means of communication among individuals of a species. Signaling pheromones trigger a specific behavior. Priming pheromones induce a physiologic change.

Positive reinforcement — A positive stimulus following a response. The strength of the response should increase as a result.

Primiparous — First-time mother; multiparous refers to subsequent maternal experiences.

Punishment — An aversive stimulus following a response. The strength of the response should decrease as a result.

Separation anxiety — Behavioral disturbance related to separation from a closely bonded relative or companion.

Sensitization — A simple form of learning involving increased response to repeated occurrence of a stimuli.

Shaping — Gradual modification of behavior by reinforcement of successive approximations of a desired behavior or sequence.

Social facilitation — "Contagious" stimulation of a particular behavior in a group of animals.

Socialization — Shaping of individual characteristics and behavior through the experience of social interaction among animals of the same species.

Spontaneous erection and penile movements — A normal behavior of male equids (and other species) involving periodic, non-sexual erection and rhythmic movements of the penis, often called masturbation.

Stereotypie — Repetitive, highly stylized, seemingly functionless motor responses and sequences, including locomotor, oral, and self-mutilative behaviors.

Vomeronasal organ (also known as Jacobson's organ) — A secondary olfactory sensory organ involved with detection of non-volatile chemicals.

Weaving — Repeated rhythmic shifting of the fore body from side to side.

Wind sucking — A term sometimes used for cribbing. (The term is also used for aspiration of air into the vagina.)

RECOMMENDED READINGS

Budiansky, S. *The Nature of Horses*. New York: Simon and Schuster, 1997.

Crowell-Davis, SL, Houpt, KA. *The Veterinary Clinics of North America, Equine Practice Volume 2: Behavior*. Philadelphia: W B Saunders and Company, 1986.

Grier, JW, Burk, T. *Biology of Animal Behavior* 3rd ed. New York: McGraw-Hill, 1999.

Hart, BL. *The Behavior of Domestic Animals*. New York: W H Freeman and Company, 1985.

Heyes, CM, Bennett GG. *Social Learning in Animals*. New York: Academic Press, 1996.

Keiper, RR. *The Assateague Ponies*. Centerville, Maryland: Tidewater Publishers, 1985.

Martin, P, Bateson, P. *Measuring Behaviour* 2nd ed. New York: Cambridge University Press, 1993.

McGreevy, P. *Why Does My Horse...?* North Pomfret, Vermont: Trafalger Square Publishing, 1996.

McCall, CA. (1990) A review of learning in horses and its application to horse training. *Journal of Animal Science* 68: p 75-81.

Walther, FR. *Communication and Expression in Hoofed Mammals*. Bloomington, Indiana: Indiana University Press, 1984.

Waring, G. *Horse Behavior*. Park Ridge, New Jersey: Noyes Publications, 1983.

Horse behavior sites on the Internet

The Horse:Your Online Guide To Equine Health Care:
http://www.thehorse.com

The American Association of Equine Practitioner's archived list
    of horse articles, which includes behavior problems:
http://www.aaep.org/client.htm

A site on equine behavior, vices, and horse psychology, and
    wild horses:
http://www.neosoft.com/~iaep/pages/animalscience/
    behavior/index.html

A forum for equine behavior questions and answers:
http://www.horsenet.com/overfence/QAbehave.html

Another equine behavior forum, a place to read about and ex-
    change equine behavior questions and answers:
http://www.gla.ac.uk/External/EBF/

The Equine Research Foundation's homepage.The
    Foundation's purpose is to further scientific and public
    knowledge about equine learning abilities:
http://members.aol.com/equiresf/horse.html

The American Veterinary Medical Association's list of equine
    web sites, including equine behavior sites:
http://www.avma.org/netvet/horses.htm

University of California, Davis' Book of Horses web site.This
    site allows for an overview of the book, which covers all
    aspects of horse care and ownership:
http://www.vetnet.ucdavis.edu/ceh/horsebook.html

Picture Credits

CHAPTER 1
Sue McDonnell, 14, 19, 20, 25; Samantha Murray, 15;
Elizabeth Ewaskiewicz, 17; Jennifer Plebani, 19, 21; Tom Hall, 22.

CHAPTER 2
Anne M. Eberhardt, 27, 28, 29, 31; Barbara D. Livington, 28.

CHAPTER 3
Anne M. Eberhardt, 32, 34, 39.

CHAPTER 4
Cheryl Manista, 43; Anne M. Eberhardt, 45, 46.

CHAPTER 5
Cheryl Manista, 48; Sue McDonnell, 50, 53; Anne M. Eberhardt, 54;
Suzie Picou-Oldham, 57.

CHAPTER 6
Sue McDonnell, 61, 65, 66, 67, 68, 70-72; Anne M. Eberhardt, 63, 67, 69, 73;
Kim and Kari Baker, 66; Samantha Murray, 68; Barbara D. Livingston, 67.

CHAPTER 7
Barbara D. Livingston, 75; Christine M. Schweizer, 77;
Anne M. Eberhardt, 79, 85; Tom Hall, 81;
Margorzata Pozor, 87.

EDITOR — JACQUELINE DUKE
COVER/BOOK DESIGN — SUZANNE C. DEPP
ILLUSTRATIONS — ROBIN PETERSON
COVER PHOTO — KATEY BARRETT

About the Author

Sue McDonnell is a native Pennsylvanian, raised in a dairy farming family in the anthracite coal regions north of Scranton. She holds a 1982 master's degree in psychology from West Chester University and a 1985 PhD in reproductive physiology and behavior from the University of Delaware. She completed post doctoral study in clinical veterinary re-

Sue McDonnell, PhD

production with Dr. Bob Kenney at the University of Pennsylvania's New Bolton Center in 1987 and became board certified in applied animal behavior in 1991.

She is the founder of the Equine Behavior Program at the University of Pennsylvania School of Veterinary Medicine, where her work includes clinical, research, and teaching activities focused on horse behavior. Dr. McDonnell is known internationally for her research-based scientific approach to equine behavior. She has conducted studies for The National Institutes of Health on the physiology and pharmacology of erection and ejaculation in horses and men. She also has studied equids throughout the world.

Dr. McDonnell maintains a semi-feral herd of ponies specifically for the study of their physiology and behavior under semi-natural conditions. This affords veterinary and animal behavior students the opportunity for long-term observation of equine social and developmental behavior and for first-hand comparison of horse behavior under free-running and traditional domestic conditions. One of Dr. McDonnell's proudest accomplishments is an honorary doctorate from The Agricultural University of Krakow, Poland, awarded for contributions toward international collaboration in equine research. Her professional hobbies include watching people and their horses as they work and play together, toward an objective understanding of the equine-human bond.